Writing for a purpose

impact

WRITING HOMEWORK

Published by Scholastic Ltd,
Villiers House,
Clarendon Avenue,
Leamington Spa,
Warwickshire CV32 5PR

© 1996 Scholastic Ltd
1 2 3 4 5 6 7 8 9 6 7 8 9 0 1 2 3 4 5

Activities by the IMPACT Project at the University of North London, collated and rewritten by Ruth Merttens, Alan Newland and Susie Webb.

UNIVERSITY OF NORTH LONDON

Editor Jane Bishop
Assistant editor Sally Gray
Designer Claire Belcher
Series designer Anna Oliwa
Illustrations Garry Davies and James Alexander
Cover illustration Hardlines, Charlbury, Oxford

Designed using Aldus Pagemaker
Printed in Great Britain by Clays Ltd, Bungay, Suffolk
British Library Cataloguing-in-Publication Data
A catalogue record for this book is available from the British Library.

ISBN 0-590-53375-4

All rights reserved. This book is sold subject to the condition that it shall not, by way of trade or otherwise, be lent, hired out or otherwise circulated without the publisher's prior consent in any form of binding or cover other than that in which it is published and without a similar condition, including this condition, being imposed upon the subsequent purchaser.

No part of this publication may be reproduced, stored in a retrieval system, or transmitted, in any form or by any means, electronic, mechanical, photocopying, recording or otherwise, without the prior permission of the publisher. This book remains copyright, although permission is granted to copy pages 6 to 10; 13 to 47; 50 to 86 and 89 to 127 for classroom distribution and use only in the school which has purchased the book, or by the teacher who has purchased this book and in accordance with the CLA licensing agreement. Photocopying permission is given for purchasers only and not for borrowers of books from any lending service.

Extract from Henry King from CAUTIONARY VERSES published by Random House 1993. Reprinted by permission of the Peters Fraser & Dunlop Group Ltd.

Crown copyright is reproduced with the permission of the Controller of HMSO.

KEY STAGE ONE
CONTENTS

Introduction	5–6
Parents' letter	6
Parents' booklet	7–10

Reception
Teachers' notes	11–12
Nursery rhyme character	13
Getting ready for snow!	14
Don't forget your bucket and spade	15
Best ever toy	16
Remember	17
Be my guest	18
Ex libris	19
Postcard!	20
Me!	21
Letter lists	22
What film?	23
Name jigsaw	24
Furniture labels	25
Name that person!	26
Toy tag	27
First and second name	28
Book cover	29
Bedtime message	30
Not too early, thank you	31
Wake up call!	32
Do not disturb!	33
Snack poster	34
Come to visit me!	35
No smoking!	36
Teatime	37
Treats	38
Animal list	39
Letter to Father Christmas	40
Way out	41
Holiday posters	42
Get well soon!	43
New title	44
Dinner-time!	45
Password	46
Baby names	47

Year One
Teachers' notes	48–49
Telephone message	50
PE lesson	51
Party games	52
Breakfast shopping	53
Birthdays	54
Favourite toys	55
Bossy language	56
ID card	57
Thank you note	58
Favourite kind of weather	59
Adverts	60
Film events	61
Family and friend register	62
Favourite meal	63
Bedtime	64
Be careful!	65
Firework safety	66
Animal babies	67

impact
WRITING HOMEWORK

KEY STAGE ONE
CONTENTS

Supercall	68
My house	69
Turn off the lights!	70
Card of thanks!	71
Fragile!	72
Flower power	73
Keep out!	74
TV postcard	75
Wet paint	76
Poison label	77
Certificate	78
This way up	79
Medal	80
Picnic fare	81
Stormy night!	82
Chewing string!	83
Animal caption	84
Wake up!	85
Car of the year	86

Year Two

Teachers' notes	87–88
Fantasy holiday	89
Bookmark	90
Rubbish and more rubbish	91
Traffic signs	92
Golden oldies	93
Party invitation	94
Ooh it's so irritating!	85
Crazy crazes!	96
Ice cream compendium	97
Pet care	98
Dial 999	99
A place for everything…	100
Telephone call	101
Saturday mornings	102
Favourite books	103
Television favourites	104
Review	105
Meal ratings	106
Favourite games	107
Top toy	108
Be safe!	109
Crossing the road	110
Ha ha ha!	111
Save water	112
More please	113
Cat collar	114
Luggage label	115
Excuses, excuses	116
Can't go now!	117
There's a frog in my porridge!	118
Welcome here	119
Silence	120
No free newspapers	121
Shoes off!	122
Ladies and gentleman	123
A wish, please!	124
Wake-up words	125
Good night all	126
Farewell my lovely	127
Afterword	128

impact
WRITING HOMEWORK

IMPACT INTRODUCTION

IMPACT books are designed to help teachers involve parents in children's learning to write. Through the use of interesting and specially developed writing tasks, parents can encourage and support their child's efforts as they become confident and competent writers.

The shared writing programme is modelled on the same process as the IMPACT shared maths which encompasses a non-traditional approach to homework.

This is outlined in the following diagram:

> The teacher selects a task based on the work she is doing in class. The activity may relate to the children's work in a particular topic, to the type of writing they are engaged in or to their reading.

> The teacher prepares the children for what they have to do at home. This may involve reading a particular story, playing a game or having a discussion with the children about the task.

> The children take home the activity, and share it with someone at home. This may be an older brother/sister, a parent or grandparent or any other friend or relation.

> The parents and children respond to the activity by commenting in an accompanying diary or notebook.
> * This mechanism provides the teacher with valuable feedback.

> The teacher uses what was done at home as the basis for follow-up work in class. This may involve further writing, drawing, reading or discussion.

The activities in this book have been designed to enable children to develop and expand their writing skills in conversation with those at home. Where possible the activities reflect the context of the home rather than the school, and draw upon experiences and events from out-of-school situations.

Shared activities – or homework with chatter!

Importantly, the activities are designed to be shared. Unlike traditional homework, where the child is expected to 'do it alone' and not to have help, with IMPACT they are encouraged – even required – to find someone to talk to and share the activity with. With each task we say the following should be true:
- something is said;
- something is written;
- something is read.

Sometimes the main point of the IMPACT activity is the discussion – and so we do try to encourage parents to see that the task involves a lot more than just completing a piece of writing. It is very important that teachers go through the task carefully with the children so that they know what to do. Clearly not all the children, or parents, will be able to read the instructions in English and so this preparation is crucial if the children are to be able to share the activity. The sheet often acts more as a backup or a prompt than a recipe.

Diaries

The shared writing works by involving parents in their children's learning. The IMPACT diaries* are a crucial part of this process. They provide a mechanism by means of which an efficient parent-teacher-dialogue is established. These diaries enable teachers to obtain valuable feedback both about children's performances in relation to specific activities and about the tasks themselves. Parents are able to alert the teacher to any matter of concern or pleasant occurrences, and nothing is left to come as a big surprise or a horrible shock in the end of year report. It is difficult to exaggerate the importance of the IMPACT diaries. The OFSTED inspectors and HMI have highly commended their effectiveness in helping to raise children's achievements and in developing a real partnership with parents.
* See the Afterword (page 128) for details of where to obtain these.

Timing

Most schools send the Shared Writing activities fortnightly. Many interleave these activities with the IMPACT maths tasks, thus ensuring that the children have something to share with their parents almost every week. Many schools also use the shared writing tasks to enhance their shared reading or PACT programme. It has been found that some parents may be encouraged to take a renewed interest in reading a book with their child on a regular basis when the shared writing project is launched in a class. However, there are a variety of practices and the important point is that each teacher should feel comfortable with how often IMPACT is sent in her class.

Parent friendly

It is important for the success of the IMPACT Shared Writing that parents are aware of both the purpose and the extent of each activity. Many teachers adopt a developmental approach to writing, encouraging emergent writing or the use of invented spellings. Care has to be taken to share the philosophy behind this approach with parents, and to select activities which will not assume that parents are as familiar with the implications as teachers. You will get lots of support if parents can see that what they are doing is helping their child to become cheerful and successful writers!

To facilitate this process, each activity contains a note to parents which helps to make it clear what the purpose of the activity is, and how they can best help. The activities also contain hints to help parents share the activity in an enjoyable and effective manner. Sometimes the hints contain ideas, or starting points. On other occasions they may be examples or demonstrations of how to set about the task concerned.

It is always important to bear in mind that parents can, and sometimes should, do things differently at home. At home, many children will enjoy, and even benefit from, copying underneath a line of text or writing without paying attention to spelling or punctuation, where in school such things might not be expected or encouraged. The most successful partnerships between home and school recognise both the differences and the similarities in each other's endeavours.

Planning

The shared writing activities are divided into three sections according to age: Reception, Year 1 and Year 2. There are two pages of teachers' notes relating to the individual activities at the beginning of each section. When selecting which activity to send home with the children it is helpful to remember the following:

- Ideally, we send the same activity with each child in the class or year. The activities are mostly designed to be as open-ended as possible, to allow for a wide variety of different levels of response. Teachers often add a few extra comments of their own to a particular sheet to fit it to the needs of a particular child or group of children with special educational needs. It is also important to stress that the child does not have to do all the actual writing – often the parent does half or more. The point of the activity may lie in the discussion and the creation of a joint product.
- It is useful to send a variety of different activities. Some children will particularly enjoy a word game, while others will prefer a task which includes drawing a picture. Activities may be used to launch a topic, to support a particular project, to enable a good quality of follow-up to an idea and to revise or practise particular skills. Much of the benefit of the shared writing exercise may be derived from the follow-up work back in the classroom. Therefore, it is very important to select activities which will feed into the type of work being focused upon at that time. For example, if the class is working on grammatical categories, verbs, nouns, etc., then an activity requiring that children and parents produce real and fictional definitions of long words will fit in well. On the other hand, if the class is doing some work on fairy stories, making a **wanted** poster of a character in a story may be appropriate.

Notes to teachers

These give suggestions to the teachers. They outline what may be done before the activity is sent to ensure that it goes well at home. And they describe how the activity may be followed up as part of routine classwork during the subsequent week. More help with what happens when the activity comes back is to be found in the Afterword on page 128.

Parent letter and booklet

It is very important that parents are kept informed about the nature of this new-style homework. Most schools elect to launch IMPACT Shared Writing by having a meeting or a series of meetings. We have included here a draft letter to parents and a booklet which schools may photocopy and give to parents. The booklet is eight A5 pages when copied, folded and collated. This can be given to all new parents as their children start school. There is a space on the cover for the school name.

Keeping shared writing going...

There are a few tips which have been found over the years to make life simpler for parents, teachers and children:

- Don't send shared writing activities in the first few weeks of the September term. Shared writing, like IMPACT maths, usually starts in the third week of the new school year.
- Don't send shared writing activities in the second half of the summer term. Shared writing, like IMPACT maths, usually belongs to the heart of the school year.
- Do value the work that the children and their parents do at home. Sometimes it may not be presented as you expect – for example, a lot of parents with young children write in upper case rather than lower case letters or will ask children to **write over** a line of print. Remember that what comes back into class is a starting point for work that you consider appropriate, and is facilitating both discussion and partnership.

Dear Parents,

In our class, we have decided to use a new 'shared homework scheme' designed to help develop and improve children's writing skills. This will involve sending home a regular task in the form of an A4 sheet. The sheet will outline a simple writing activity for you and your child to enjoy together. These are designed to be shared; the children are not expected to complete the tasks alone.

We would very much like to talk to you about this scheme, and so on _____ we shall hold three short meetings. You need only come to **one** of these and can choose the time which is most convenient:

- 9.00 in the morning
- 3.30 in the afternoon
- 7.00 in the evening.

We would really like as many parents as possible to attend.

Your help in supporting your child's learning is a crucial part of his/her success at school. We do appreciate the time and trouble that parents take with their children, and we can certainly see the benefits in the quality of the children's work and the enthusiasm with which they attack it.

Please return the slip at the bottom of the letter.

Yours sincerely,

_____

Name _____   Class _____

I would like to attend the meeting at:

9.00 in the morning

3.30 in the afternoon

7.00 in the evening

Please tick **one** time only.

Don't forget...

Pick your time!
When you both want to do the activity.

Don't over-correct!
This can be very discouraging.

Your child does not always have to do all the writing!
You may take turns, or take over sometimes.

Make it fun!
If either of you gets tired or bored help a bit more. Tasks should not last more than 20 minutes unless you want them to!

Praise and encourage as much as you can!

IMPACT

Shared Writing

SPIKE

School name

_____

About Shared Writing

- The teacher selects an activity
- The teacher explains the activity to the class.
- Child and helper read through the activity.
- Child and helper talk about the activity.
- Child and helper share the writing.
- Child and helper comment on the activity in the diary.
- Child brings the activity back into school.
- Teacher reads the comments in the diary.
- The teacher follows up the activity in class.

Spelling and punctuation

We all agree that correct spelling and punctuation are very important. However........

DO

- Notice punctuation when sharing the writing activity.
- Talk about different uses of capital and lower case letters.
- Play word games such as 'I spy' or 'Hangman'.
- Read what the child has written before you make any comment about spelling, punctuation or presentation.
- Help them learn any words sent home by the school.

DON'T

- Worry about every mistake – children can become very anxious about their writing if constantly interrupted.
- With young children don't insist that they spell every word correctly. At this stage we are encouraging them to 'be writers'.
- Don't worry if your child is quite slow to learn to spell and punctuate – these things come with time and encouragement.

How we write

Writing also has a mechanical side, children have to learn to form their letters, to separate words, to begin and end sentences.

When children are first learning to write it can be very discouraging to be constantly corrected. However, as they become more confident, we can afford to draw their attention to these things:

Starting school

Your child already knows quite a lot about writing when they start........

They may

• be able to tell the difference between writing and pictures;

• realise that writing has words and spaces;

• know some letters of their name;

• be able to make marks on paper or form a few letters;

• understand that 'talk' can be written down and that writing can give messages or information;

• know that we write from left to right in English;

• play at 'reading' their own 'writing'.

Teachers' Notes
RECEPTION

Nursery rhyme character Read through a selection of nursery rhymes with the children before this activity goes home. When the children bring back their character names into class, talk about the range. Is there a favourite? Has anyone thought of a really unusual character? Can the children say why they like the character? (For example Wee Willy Winkie because they like staying up late!)

Getting ready for snow! Make a display of the children's lists next to a display of the actual items of clothing. For example, you could pin up a pair of gloves, a scarf, a woolly hat, a thick pair of socks etc. Talk about how you need to be both warm and dry when playing out in the snow. Write a list of games to play outside in the snow.

Don't forget your bucket and spade! Make a display of the children's lists next to a display of the actual items the children suggest. For example, you could pin up a bucket and spade, swimming costume, sun-hat etc. Talk about how you need to be both cool and protected from the sun when playing on the beach. Write a class list of games to play on the beach.

Best ever toy! Before sending this activity home, bring in some advertisements to talk through with the children. Talk about the types of language used. Look at some slogans. When the children have drawn their adverts, discuss them all. Which ones are particularly effective? Why? Put the children in groups of four to make some advertisement 'bill boards' to advertise their favourite toys. They can work together and use paint on huge sheets of paper. Display them in the school hall!

Remember... Let the children share their notes with one another. Have any of the children decided to remind themselves of the same things? Think of some things in the classroom or school context which could need reminders.

Be my guest! Make a class book of all the children's invitations, entitled 'Guess who's coming to tea?'. Think of some really exciting people to ask into your classroom! Perhaps you can 'invite' a TV celebrity or a famous footballer! Write and illustrate some big invitations and display them.

Ex-libris Before the children take home this activity, provide each child with a small sticky label (available in strips from most newsagents – about 3p each). Discuss each child's choice of book. Have some children chosen the same book? The children can copy the cover of the book or draw a picture of a scene or character in the book and write the book's title beside their picture. Mount these for a display or a class book entitled 'Our favourite books'.

Postcard Before this activity goes home, staple a small plain postcard to each sheet. (From stationers in packets costing between 5p and 10p each.) When the children bring back their postcards, help them to address their cards to their friends. Put up a big list with the names of all the children in the class, and encourage them to look for the first letter to find the right name. Have some spare postcards for children to draw and write in class if necessary. Make sure that every child receives at least one card!

Me! Make a class album using a scrap book. Take a photo of each child and then stick their name, address, age and date of birth on the same page as their photo. Each child can then write a short paragraph about themselves and this can be mounted on the facing page. The children will really love to read this book, and will spend a long time studying it in pairs and on their own. The children can also make ID cards, with a small 'head and shoulders' drawing of themselves on the front and all their details on the back.

Letter lists Fill in the relevant letter on the sheet before handing it out to the children. Think up a few words that begin with your sound altogether to start the list off before this goes home. When the lists come back into class, display them on your 'sound table', the children can then use them for their work in the classroom.

What film? When the children bring back their film titles and pictures, display them and add reviews. Display the work in a book or on the wall. Talk about what they did or did not like about the film, who the film might be aimed at, and ask whether they would recommend it to someone else.

Name jigsaw Before this activity goes home, make up a 'jigsaw' of your own name. This gives the children a much better idea of what the task requires. It will also give you an opportunity to remind the children not to cut their jigsaws into too many little pieces! Remember to give each child an envelope for their pieces. When the jigsaws come back, put the children in pairs, and encourage them to each show their partner how to do their jigsaw. They can then swap, and try one another's.

Furniture labels / Name that person! / Toy tag Before these activities go home, make sure every child has blank stickers for writing their labels onto. (If you think parents might object to actual stickers, you could supply self-adhesive stickers that can be easily peeled off!) Talk about the children's labels. What could you make labels for in the class? Perhaps you could have a store of self-adhesive stickers that the children can write on, and then stick to things in the class.

First and second name Photocopy and enlarge a copy of the boxes on page 28 and fill it in with your own name. Count the number of letters with the children. When the children bring back their activity sheets, go around the class and ask the children how many letters they have in their first and last names. Who has the longest name? Who has the longest first or last name? Are the children able to sort the names into initial sound groups?

Book cover Before this activity goes home look at plenty of books together and study the covers. Look at interesting ways of writing the letters in the title and ways of decorating the letters.

Bedtime message Before this activity goes home give each child some self-adhesive stickers so that they can use these to write their message. This adds an air of realism to the whole activity and the children will be much more inclined to write a good message! When the children bring all their messages back into class, make a class book of all the messages. This can be made by sewing several folded A1 sheets of sugar paper together. The children can draw or paint pictures of themselves in bed to go with their message. Remind them to include any teddy bears they take to bed. The children will love reading their book, especially if you write a few comments for each child throughout the book.

Not too early, thank you! Make a display of all the children's signs. Group the signs according to what time the children get up! Use the activity to start a discussion about time – ask the children at roughly what time do we get up? Go to bed? Eat tea? Come to school? The children can draw a picture of what they like to do as soon as they wake up, when it is *not* a school day!

Wake up call! Display the best signs. Discuss the time we start school, and the time we need to leave home in order to get there on time. Draw the clock faces depicting the relevant times. How do the children come to school? What do they have to eat for breakfast? Make a block graph of the children's method of transport or of their chosen breakfasts (which ever has the most variety!). Ask each child to draw a picture of themselves or to write their name on a 'block' cut out of paper or card, and they can then place it on the graph in the appropriate place.

Do not disturb! Talk about all the children's signs and discuss the different things that they might be doing where they would not like to be disturbed. Discuss different adult hobbies – reading, writing, listening to the radio, sleeping (!) where it might be important not to have too much noise. What other signs might people hang on their doors? Think about the 'No hawkers', 'No free newspapers' type signs. Make a class collection of different types of sign. Perhaps the children can make some signs for the classroom for example 'quiet corner', 'painting table' and so on.

Snack poster Make a display of all the children's posters. Discuss which types of snack were popular, and record the information on a block graph. Each child can write their name or draw a picture of themselves on a small 'block' cut out of paper or thin card, and then place it in the appropriate place on the block graph. Bring in some examples of different snacks and discuss which ones are healthy and which ones are not so. Divide them into two sets. Label the sets. Discuss when we are inclined to eat snacks (do the children bring something in for break-time?). Look at some clock-face times to match the occasions to the hours of the day (for example – 10.30 at break time or when they get in from school at 4.00).

Come to visit me! Encourage the children to talk about their invitations in class. Have they all said when the person is to come? Have they said what time? Do they mention whether there will be a meal involved? Do they say what the purpose of the visit is – for example a birthday, or a party or just to play. Discuss what must go on an invitation. When they have finished they can take their invitations back home. Perhaps some of them can actually send them out!

No smoking! Collect some real examples of 'No Smoking' signs to show the children before the activity goes home. Discuss the symbols or graphics which the signs use to convey their message. Display the children's signs around the classroom door, in the entrance hall or on the window (facing outward!) so that the parents can see them. Discuss other sorts of public sign which the children may have seen. Can they bring in some examples of these?

Teatime Discuss what each child has written and make a class list of all the things they like for their tea. Is there anything which appears on more than one list? Can they draw or paint a big 'teatime spread' picture?

Treats Discuss all the children's lists. Which things are on everyone's list? Make a block graph of the ten or twelve most popular items and let the children write their name on a block and place it in the appropriate place on the graph. Write down all the things which have been mentioned – even if only by one child – on small pieces of card and shuffle them up. Can the children recognise the word for their favourite treat? Sort the cards into two (or more) sets in different ways – for example by initial letter or by type (food/drink, savoury/sweet). Draw picture labels to go with each set.

Animal list Discuss which animals are the favourites. Make a class list of the 'top ten' animals. The children can work in pairs or small groups to paint a large picture of one of the animals on the list. Display the class list and all the paintings as well as the children's individual lists. Can the children put the animals in alphabetical order? Can they find an animal for each letter of the alphabet so that the class can produce a home-made animal frieze? Are there other ways of ordering the animals on their list – for example in order of size, smallest to largest? Make cards with the name of the animal on one side and the picture on the other. Can the children learn to read the names of all the animals?

Letter to Father Christmas Read out all the children's letters. Is anything on everyone's list or on several children's? Write a joint letter to Father Christmas. Talk about how we begin and end letters. Talk about how after Christmas, we write 'Thank you' letters. Discuss how we write these and what words they will contain. Make a class book of all the children's letters written at home or in school.

Way out Discuss the different ways the children have decided to design their signs. Talk about the fact that how the words are written is sometimes as important as what words are used. Discuss the use of symbols and icons to convey a message which could also be conveyed in words. Look at examples of 'No entry', 'Road closed', 'Hump-backed bridge', 'School' and 'Children crossing' signs and others which provide instances of this kind of graphical communication. The children can copy these signs and write down what they mean. Perhaps they can also make up some new ones of their own.

Holiday posters Display all the children's posters. Make a list of the things everyone liked – about your neighbourhood, for example the playground, the swimming pool, the local shop... Work with the children to draw a large map of the area, and pin this up. Working in pairs, the children can add pictures and words to this map, and write signs and headings to go on it.

Get well soon! Share all the cards. Discuss the sort of things the children drew and the words they used on the inside of the card. Make a class list of words to do with feeling and being ill, with hospitals and so on. Make a list of the different types of card which you see in a card shop – 'Sorry it's late', 'Happy birthday', 'Happy Easter/Christmas,' 'Valentine's day', 'Congratulations', 'Sorry', 'Thank you', and so on. Talk about the cards the children have received. Can they bring in some different types to show? Send home the 'Get well cards' so that they can be sent to all the sick friends!

New title Before sending home this activity, talk through a whole selection of programme titles with the children. Discuss the length of the titles – and how they are quite snappy! Use the children's ideas to see how well they have succeeded by reading out the new title and asking the whole class to guess the programme. Talk about the types of word used in a title.

Dinner-time! Make signs with the children's 'calls' on. Write them as speech bubbles and make a display with some favourite food wrappers.

Password Write each password on a separate piece of paper, shuffle them up and hand them out to the children at random. Can they read them? Sort the cards by their first letters or by how many letters are in each word.

Baby names Have any of the children come up with the same words? Talk about why some words are more common than others. Make a display with the childen's words in speech bubbles around some photos of the children as babies, or ask the children to make a painting of themselves.

Nursery rhyme character

Who is your favourite nursery rhyme character?

● Write down the name, and draw a picture of the character.

To the helper:

● Talk about the nursery rhymes your child knows. Do you know any that your child does not know?
● Talk about what a character is; help them choose their favourite.
● Help with the writing if your child wants you to.
● Talk about the letters in the name – can they recognise any of them?

By having to think of their favourite nursery rhyme character name, the children are being given a reason to write something down which interests them.

_____and

child

_____

helper(s)

did this activity together

impact WRITING HOMEWORK

Writing for a purpose   13

To the helper:

- Has your child ever seen snow? Talk about the last time it snowed and what it was like.
- What games can you play in the snow? What special clothes would you wear if you were going to play in the snow?
- Help with the writing if your child wants you to. They could draw pictures to remind them what the words say.

Writing lists is an essential skill in writing; it allows the children to sort and order their ideas. The purpose of writing is to record a set of ideas that the children can refer back to at a later date.

_____and
child

_____
helper(s)

_____
did this activity together

14 **Writing for a purpose**

Getting ready for snow!

Brrr!

Pretend it's going to snow soon, so let's be ready for it.

- Write a list of all the things you will need to wear to play in the snow.

impact WRITING HOMEWORK

Don't forget your bucket and spade!

Imagine the sun has come out!
Let's pretend we are going to the beach.

What do we need to take with us?

- Write a list of things to take for a day at the beach on a hot, sunny day.

To the helper:
- Has your child ever been to a beach? Talk about what it is like.
- What games can you play on the beach? For example paddling and digging. What special clothes will you need to wear to do these things?
- Help with the writing if your child wants you to. They could draw pictures to remind them what the words say.

Writing lists is an essential skill in writing; it allows the children to sort and order their ideas. The purpose of this writing is to record a set of ideas that the children can then refer back to at a later date.

_____and
child

_____
helper(s)

_____
did this activity together

impact WRITING HOMEWORK

Writing for a purpose   15

To the helper:

- Help your child by talking to them about their toy. Look at it carefully together. Discuss what is so good about it and why they like it.
- Write a descriptive line or a slogan on their advert for them!

We shall discuss the children's advertisements and the kind of language used in adverts. These call for a particular kind of writing, and we shall be looking at this in school.

_____and
child

_____
helper(s)

_____
did this activity together

16 Writing for a purpose

Best ever toy!

What's your favourite toy?

Can you make an advert for it?

● Draw a really good picture and ask your helper to help you write some words about it, or give it a new name! Can you think of a slogan?

impact WRITING HOMEWORK

Remember...

Is there something that you often forget to do?

● Draw yourself a picture to remind you.
Write a few words which will act as a reminder too!

To the helper:

● Talk to your child about something they – or you – often forget. For example perhaps they forget to take something into school. They can draw a picture of the item and write the words 'Remember book folder' beside it!

In school we shall discuss the purposes of written reminders – and how effective they can be. We are encouraging children to write by thinking about the purpose of writing.

_____and
child

_____
helper(s)

_____
did this activity together

impact WRITING HOMEWORK

Writing for a purpose   17

To the helper:

- Talk to your child about who they would like to invite.
- Encourage your child to write a short invitation – they do not need to write all the words. Perhaps they can write the name of their character and you can write the rest.

One of the main purposes of writing is to get in touch with friends via invitations, letters, cards and so on. In this activity, we are helping children realise that they too can communicate using writing.

_____and
child

_____
helper(s)

did this activity together

Writing for a purpose

Be my guest!

Which is your favourite character in a book or a programme or a film?

- Draw a picture of the character.
- Write them an invitation asking them to tea!

impact WRITING HOMEWORK

Ex-libris

Ex-libris means 'from the library of...' or 'belonging to'. Some people stick labels with this on in their books to show who they belong to.

Have you got a very favourite book?

- Write your name on the label provided. Decorate your label so it looks nice. Stick it on the front page of your favourite book.

- Bring your book into school.

To the helper:

- Talk to your child about which book they like, and why.
- Help them to write their name if necessary.
- If they can write their first name easily, ask them to write their surname as well!

Labels are useful and they provide a reason to have to write clearly and legibly. This activity reinforces the children's knowledge of how to write their name.

_____and
child

_____
helper(s)

_____

did this activity together

Writing for a purpose

To the helper:

- Talk to your child about who they are going to send the postcards to at school. Discuss what picture they should draw on the front.
- Help them to write a message – they could write the name of the person the postcard is for, and some of the message.

Postcards and letters provide a very practical purpose for writing. This activity helps children to realise that their writing helps them to communicate with someone.

_____ and
child

_____
helper(s)

did this activity together

Postcard!

We are going to send postcards to our friends.

- Draw a picture on the front of your card. Make sure it is a really good picture – perhaps of somewhere you have been, or something you have done over the weekend!

- Write a message on the back with your helper. Sign the postcard with your name.

20 **Writing for a purpose**

impact WRITING HOMEWORK

Me!

We are collecting information about ourselves!

We need to know about you.

Name _____

Address _____

_____

_____

_____

Age _____

Date of birth _____

- Fill in this form and bring it in to school.

To the helper:

- Talk to your child about how they are going to write this information. How do we write an address? They will need help with this.

It is very helpful for children to learn how to provide this type of information about themselves. Writing our names and addresses is not easy – there are so many conventions. We are learning about these in class.

_____ and
child

_____
helper(s)

_____
did this activity together

impact WRITING HOMEWORK

Writing for a purpose   21

To the helper:

- Talk about the sound the letter makes. Can you brainstorm any words that begin with that sound?

This is the sound that the children are focusing on at school this week. We shall use the initial sound lists as a resource in the classroom.

_____ and

child

_____

helper(s)

did this activity together

Letter lists

This week's letter is _____

- Write down a list of things with your helper that start with that letter.

22 **Writing for a purpose**

impact WRITING HOMEWORK

What film?

Have you seen any films recently?

- Write down the name of the film and draw a picture.

To the helper:

- Talk about any films you have seen. Your child might choose one which you saw together, or one your child saw with friends at the cinema, on video or on the television.

Back at school we shall be talking about films we have seen, and which were the best films we have seen and why. This provides the children with a purpose for writing on a topic which is relevant to them.

_____ and
child

_____
helper(s)

_____
did this activity together

Writing for a purpose

To the helper:

- Talk about each letter in your child's name.
- When you cut up the jigsaw, try not to create too many pieces! One or maybe two pieces per letter is enough.
- Play with the jigsaw at home before your child takes it to school. How quickly can you put it together? How quickly can someone else in your house put it together?

This is one of the many ways you can use to help children become more familiar with their own names. We shall play with the jigsaws at school; looking at how the letters are ordered and go together.

_____and
child

_____
helper(s)

_____
did this activity together

24 **Writing for a purpose**

Name jigsaw

- Write your name in big letters in this box.
- Now decorate it with bright colours.
- Cut it into pieces so that it makes a jigsaw.
Put all the pieces into your envelope, and bring it to school.

impact WRITING HOMEWORK

Furniture labels

● Use your stickers to make name labels for your three favourite pieces of furniture. For example, your bed, the television and a really comfy chair.

To the helper:

● Once they have chosen what to make the labels for, the children can write the name of the piece of furniture ('chair') on a label, and then stick it on.

Labelling is an important and useful purpose for writing. We shall be making some more labels for things in the classroom.

_____and
child

_____
helper(s)

_____
did this activity together

Writing for a purpose

To the helper:

- Help your child with the writing of the name labels. The children can write the person's name on a label, and then stick it on. (It might be an idea to ask before you stick!)

Labelling is an important and useful purpose for writing. We shall be making some more labels for things in the classroom.

_____ and
child

_____
helper(s)

_____
did this activity together

26   **Writing for a purpose**

Name that person!

Use the stickers to make name labels for your family.

● Write the name on a label and stick it on the right person!

impact WRITING HOMEWORK

Toy tag

● Use the stickers to make name labels for your three favourite toys. For example, your teddy, the computer, and your favourite game.

To the helper:

● Help your child with the writing of the toys labels, once they have chosen which toys to make them for. The idea is that the children write the name of the toy on each label, and then stick it on.

Labelling is an important and useful purpose for writing. We shall be making some more labels for things in the classroom.

_____and
child

_____
helper(s)

_____
did this activity together

Writing for a purpose

To the helper:

- Help your child put a letter in each box – they may forget what order the letters in their name are if they are concentrating too hard on the boxes!
- Talk about the letters in your child's second name together; have you ever looked really closely at it before?

Separating and scrutinising the letters in a child's name gives an opportunity to look closely at the order of letters, and will help with spelling it in the future. We shall be comparing how many letters are in each other's names at school.

_____and

child

_____

helper(s)

_____

did this activity together

28 Writing for a p...

First and second name

- Write your first name, and second name in these boxes. Make sure that you only put one letter in each box!

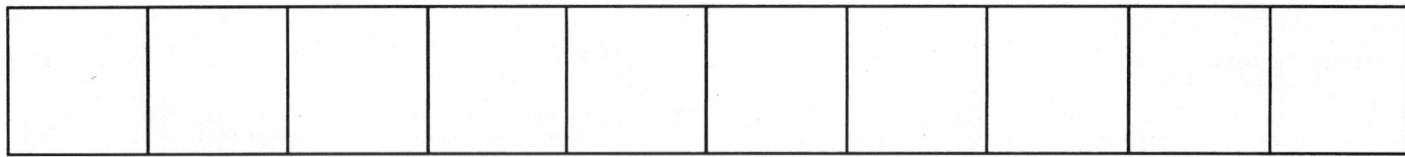

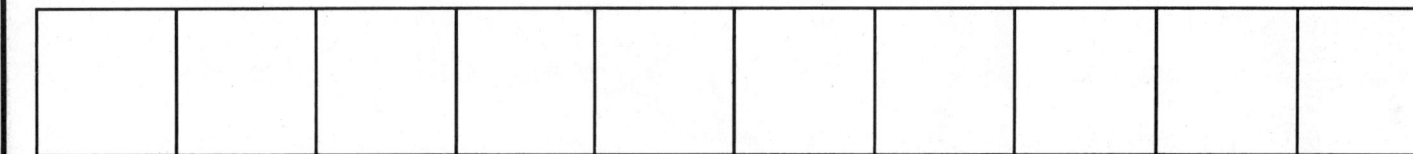

Now count how many letters there are altogether in your name.

impact WRITING HOMEWORK

Book cover

- Can you design a cover for a book?
- Give your book a title and draw a picture.

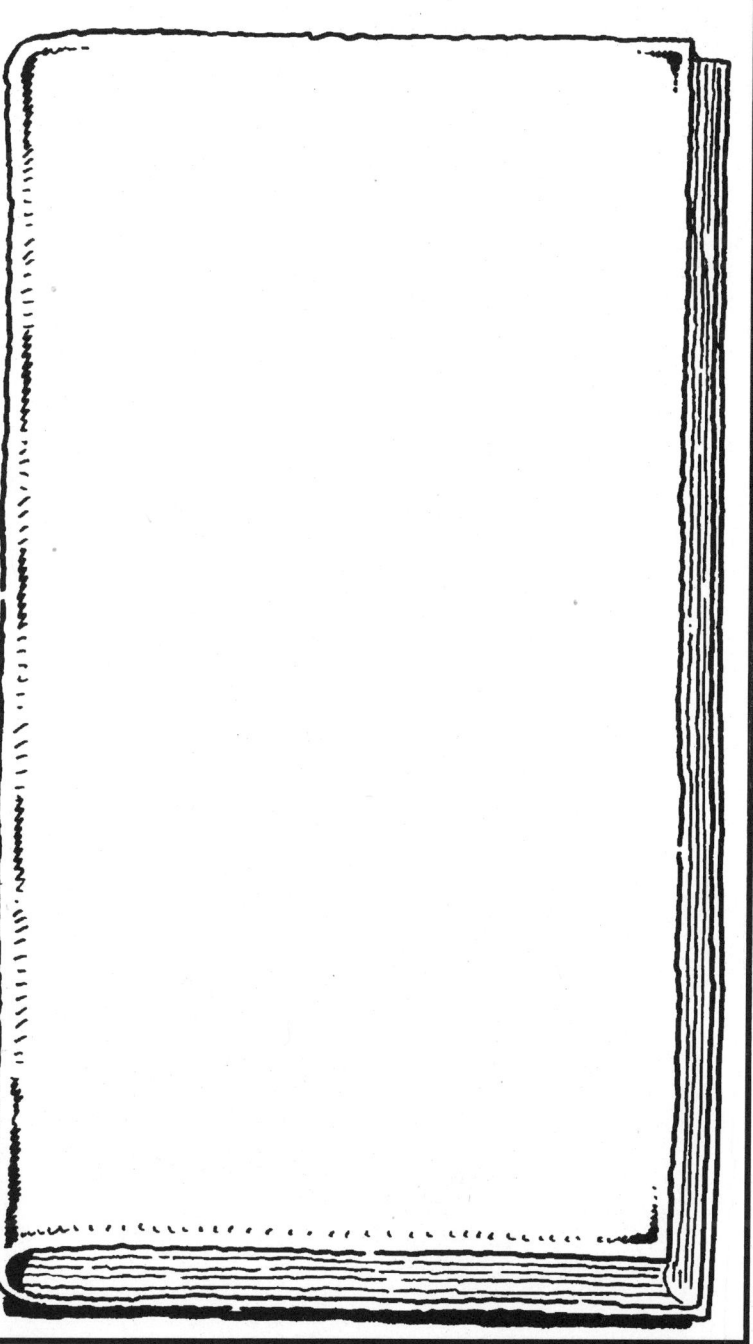

To the helper:

- Look at some book covers together. What information is given, for example, publisher, author, title, price...
- Help your child to design their cover in the same way.

Designing a book cover provides a purpose for writing. It will also help develop the child's awareness of what information needs to be given in this context.

_____and
child

_____
helper(s)

_____
did this activity together

Writing for a purpose

To the helper:

- This only needs to be a short note, as long as the message gets across. It could be communicated through pictures, symbols and words.
- If your child needs help with the words, then give the help needed.

The skill of writing comprehensible messages is an important one which will be used in the future.

_____ and

child

_____

helper(s)

_____

did this activity together

30   Writing for a purpose

Bedtime message

Who is going to put you to bed tonight?

- Write a message to the person saying what time you would like to go to bed.

impact WRITING HOMEWORK

Not too early, thank you!

What time are you allowed to wake other people up in your house?

- Make a sign that will help you remember.

To the helper:

- Talk about the purpose of these kind of signs, and where you might see them.
- Your child could use some of the writing on this sheet to help with the spelling on the sign.

Making signs will help children be clear about what they write and draw. It helps them to learn to use precise language.

_____and
child

_____
helper(s)

_____
did this activity together

impact WRITING HOMEWORK

Writing for a purpose 31

To the helper:

- Talk about the purpose of these kinds of signs.
- Your child could use some of the words on this sheet to help with the spelling on their sign.

Writing signs will help children be clear about what they write and draw. It helps them to learn to use precise language.

_____ and
child

_____
helper(s)

_____
did this activity together

32 **Writing for a purpose**

Wake up call!

- Design a sign to hang on your bedroom door.

It should tell someone to wake you up in time for school!

- Decorate it with crayons or felt-tipped pens.

impact WRITING HOMEWORK

Do not disturb!

Make a 'Do not disturb' notice to hang on your door.

● Draw a picture of something you would like to do when you would not like to be disturbed on your sign.

To the helper:
● Talk about the purpose of 'Do not disturb' signs, and where you might see them.
● Your child could use the writing on this sheet to help with the spelling of 'Do not disturb'.

Writing signs will help children be clear about what they write and draw. It helps them to learn to use precise language.

_____ and
child

_____
helper(s)

_____
did this activity together

impact WRITING HOMEWORK

Writing for a purpose 33

To the helper:

- Discuss your child's favourite snack; what is so delicious about it? You can help with the writing as much as your child needs you to.
- Make sure that the name of the product/food, and the picture are both clear.

Making posters is one form of writing for a purpose. A certain message has to be communicated clearly, and attractively. We shall display the children's poster at school.

_____ and
child

_____
helper(s)

_____
did this activity together

Snack poster

What is your favourite snack?

- Make a poster about it.
- Draw a picture, and write down all the good things about it.

34 **Writing for a purpose**

impact WRITING HOMEWORK

Come to visit me!

Invite someone to visit you.

- Write an invitation to someone you like, asking them to come and see you.

Don't forget to tell the date and time!

Decorate your invitation.

To the helper:

- Talk to your child about who they would like to invite. Encourage them to choose someone who might be able to accept!
- Help your child to write a short invitation – they do not need to write all the words. Perhaps they can write the name of the friend and you can write the rest?

One of the main purposes of writing is to get in touch with our friends via invitations, letters, cards and so on. In this activity, we are showing the children that they too can use writing to communicate.

_____and
child

_____
helper(s)

_____
did this activity together

Writing for a purpose 35

To the helper:

● Talk about the purposes of these kinds of signs, and where you might see them. Point out the 'No smoking' sign shown here. Your sign should convey the same message, but in a different way.
● Your child could use some of the writing on this sheet to help with the spelling on the sign.

Making signs will help children be clear about what they write and draw. It helps them to learn to use precise language.

_____and

child

_____

helper(s)

_____

did this activity together

36   Writing for a purpose

No smoking!

Can you make a 'No smoking' sign?

What will your sign look like?

● Design it so it will work!

impact WRITING HOMEWORK

Teatime

What's your favourite thing for tea?

● Write a message to say one thing that you would like to have for tea tomorrow.

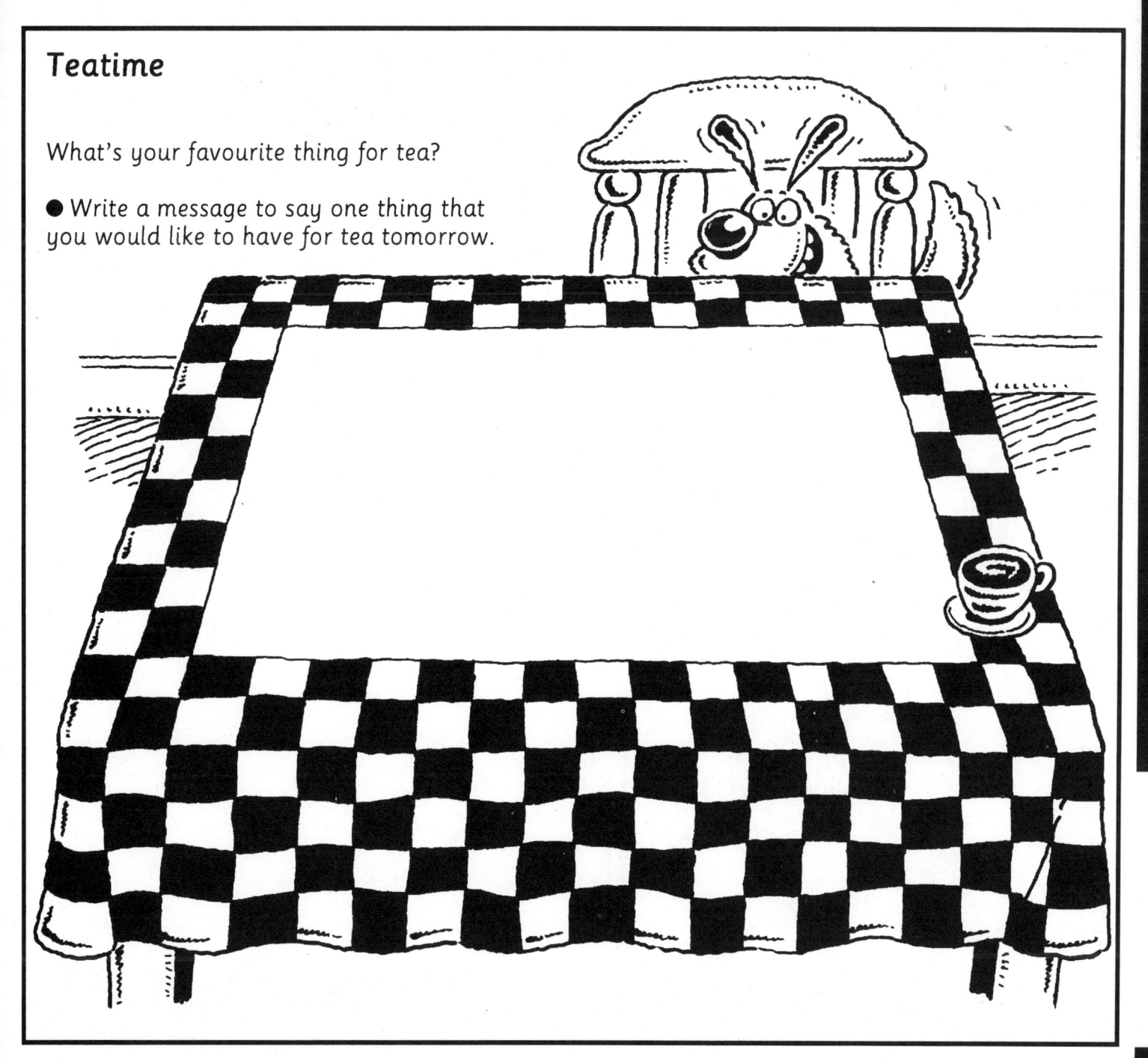

To the helper:

● This only needs to be short. It could be communicated through pictures, symbols or words.
● If your child needs help with the words, then give the help needed.

The skill of writing comprehensible messages is an important one which will be needed in the future.

_____ and
child

_____
helper(s)

_____
did this activity together

impact WRITING HOMEWORK

Writing for a purpose

To the helper:

- Talk about the kinds of things your child enjoys for treats.
- This list could be part-written, and part-diagrams if your child finds that easier.
- Give a hand with any writing if necessary.

Writing lists is an essential skill in writing; it allows the children to sort and order their ideas. The purpose of this writing is to record a set of ideas that the children can then refer back to at a later date.

_____ and
child

_____
helper(s)

_____
did this activity together

Writing for a purpose

Treats

- Write a list of three things you would like someone to buy you for a treat.

For example: ice cream, chocolate flake, fizzy drink.

- Draw one of your treats.

impact WRITING HOMEWORK

Animal list

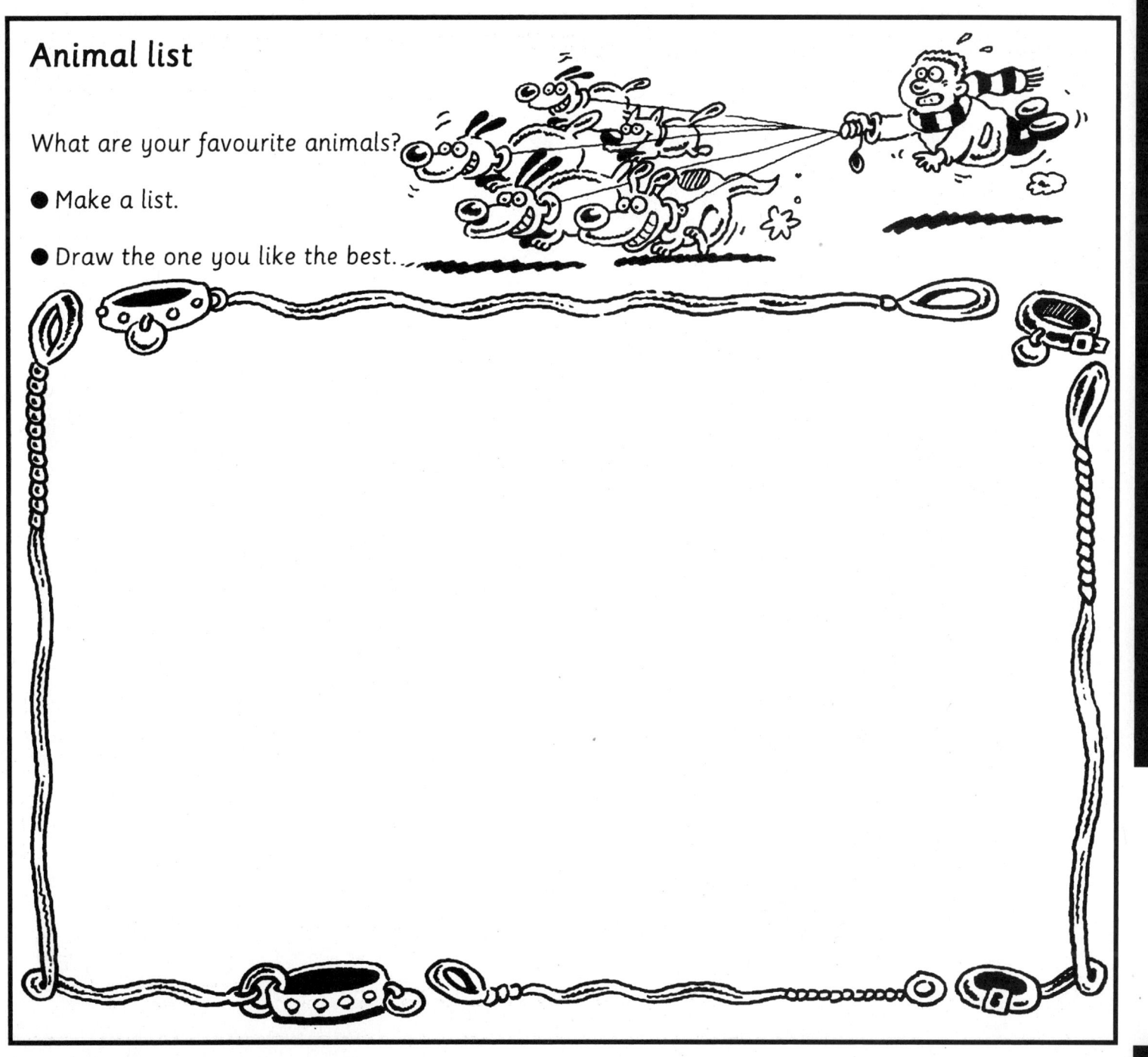

What are your favourite animals?

- Make a list.
- Draw the one you like the best.

To the helper:

- Help your child decide what their favourite animals are.
- Give a hand with the writing if needed.

Writing lists is an essential skill in writing; it allows the children to sort and order their ideas. The purpose of this writing is to record a set of ideas that the children can then refer back to at a later date. We shall talk about the animals at school.

_____and

child

_____

helper(s)

_____

did this activity together

impact WRITING HOMEWORK

Writing for a purpose 39

To the helper:

- Talk about what your child would like for Christmas.
- Talk about how a letter is written. You could share the writing with you writing the main part of the letter, while your child writes (with your help) the 'Dear Father Christmas' and 'Love from ____' parts.

Writing letters and notes are important forms of writing that the children will need to be familiar with. We shall discuss the children's letters at school.

_____ and
child

_____
helper(s)

_____
did this activity together

40 **Writing for a purpose**

Letter to Father Christmas

● Write a letter to Father Christmas saying what you would like for Christmas.

Bring it to school before you send it!

impact WRITING HOMEWORK

Way out

- Make an 'Exit' or 'Way out' sign for your home.

To the helper:

- Talk about the purpose of these kind of signs, and where you might see them.
- Your child could use the writing on this sheet to help with the spelling on the sign.

Writing signs will help children be clear about what they write and draw. It helps them to learn to use precise language.

_____ and
child

_____
helper(s)

_____
did this activity together

impact WRITING HOMEWORK

Writing for a purpose 41

To the helper:

● Discuss where you live; what things might be attractive to other people? Can your child **say** what they like about it? You can help with the writing as far as necessary.

Making posters is one form of writing for a purpose. A certain message has to be communicted clearly, and attractively. We shall display the children's posters at school.

_____and
child

_____
helper(s)

_____
did this activity together

42 **Writing for a purpose**

Holiday posters

Do you live in a nice place?

Imagine that people might want to come there on holiday! Think of all the good things about living where you do.

● Design a colourful poster of the place where you live.

impact WRITING HOMEWORK

Get well soon!

Is someone you know feeling unwell?

- Make them a 'Get well soon' card.

To the helper:
- Help your child b... discussing which programme th... and why?
- Talk a... happen... to b...

...to school befor... it to the person you made it for.

This activity will help the children focus on one of the ways in which writing is important and useful in real life.

_____ and
child

_____
helper(s)

did this activity together

impact WRITING HOMEWORK

Writing for a purpose   43

New title

What is your favourite TV programme?

- Give it a new title! Think of a new title for it and write this down.
- Draw a picture of something to do with this programme.

...y

...ey like best

...bout what
...ns in the programme
...elp your child invent a
...new title. Remember a title
should be short.

We shall discuss all the children's new titles in class. The children will try to guess what the old title of the programme was by hearing the new title! This will help focus their attention on some of the descriptive features of the programme.

_____and
child

_____
helper(s)

did this activity together

44   **Writing for a purpose**

impact WRITING HOMEWORK

Dinner-time!

When your meals are ready how do you like to be called to come and eat?

Would you like someone to ring a bell or a gong? Do you like to know what you are being called to eat?

Shepherd's pie, Jamie!

● Write down your favourite food-time call!

To the helper:

● Discuss this together and help to write down your child's favourite way of being called (which may involve a favourite meal or even food!).

This activity gives children a reason to think about and write a short sentence or phrase which they may hear spoken but have never seen written down.

_____and
child

_____
helper(s)

_____
did this activity together

impact WRITING HOMEWORK

Writing for a purpose   45

To the helper:

- Talk to your child about passwords. Describe some of the situations in which they might be used – for a secret 'club', during a war or on a computer. Help them write their password. How will they spell it?

Often children find the whole idea of passwords very exciting. We shall discuss the idea that words can 'open doors' and do some more writing around this topic in class.

_____and
child

_____
helper(s)

_____
did this activity together

Writing for a purpose

Password

Sometimes people use passwords so that only the people who know it can get into (or out of!) somewhere special!

- Think of a password of your own.

- Write it down.

When would you use it?

impact WRITING HOMEWORK

Baby names

When babies learn to talk they often use words which are not quite right.

Have you ever heard a baby call something by the wrong name? Can anyone remember any words which you said when you were a baby which were not quite right?

- Write a list of two or three of the words you used to say when you were a baby.

To the helper:

- Talk to your child about the sorts of things that they used to say when they were little. Can you remember two or three? You may need to help write these odd words down!

This activity will make the children think about the sound of the words and how they might be written. Writing lists is also a very useful activity.

_____ and

child

_____

helper(s)

_____

did this activity together

impact WRITING HOMEWORK

Writing for a purpose 47

Teachers' Notes
YEAR ONE

Telephone message To practise this try a role-play where someone (you) rings up one of the children and they must take a message. Suggest what kind of message it might be – good news, bad news or a reminder. When the children bring back their messages, see if they can remember what the point of the message was. Would somebody else be able to read their message?

PE lesson Discuss the kinds of things you can do in a PE session. When the children's ideas come back in collect them and use them for a lesson. Stick the children's ideas up around the hall or PE area. Start off two or three children at each point. They must read the instruction, carry it out, and then move on to the next one.

Party games Has anyone chosen a game that no-one else knows? Ask the children to explain the rules for their games. Carry out a class survey to find out which were the favourite games. Perhaps you could plan a small party (at the end of term/year) and make party invitations, food and play their favourite games!

Breakfast shopping Read *The Tiger who Came to Tea* by Judith Kerr (Picture Lions) to the children before this activity goes home. After the activity discuss the types of things that the tiger ate from their house. Make 'The tiger who came to breakfast' books, using their ideas for the things that he came to eat. The children can draw their own illustrations.

Birthdays Sort the children into groups according to which month their birthday is. Give each child a piece of card with the date of their birthday on, so for example Sarah (28th February) stands in the February group, holding a card with 28 on it. Then ask the children to get themselves in order; from the beginning of the month to the end. You can then fill everyone's birthday dates in on the calendar.

Favourite toys Do some children share favourites? Make a block graph with the type of toy along the bottom axis and the number of children who liked that toy indicated for each column. The blocks can consist of the children's drawings of each toy in a standard block cut out of paper. Encourage the children to describe their toys. What descriptive words do they use? Make a list of the words. Some of the children can write stories about their toys, or they can write a description to go with their drawing.

Bossy language! Compare all the children's instructions. Have several of the children given instructions for the same task, for example teeth-cleaning? Have they broken down the task into the same steps? Is their order always the same? Talk about whether the order in which you do things matters and why. Write some instructions for a task, cut each instruction out and muddle up the order. Can the children put them back into the right order?

ID card Use the information for a range of maths activities. The ID cards themselves can be displayed in a 'rogue's gallery' which all the children can enjoy.

Thank you note Before the activity goes home, talk about the kind of thing they might write about. Remind them that this is a note it does not have to be a perfect letter. When the ideas come back back, talk about the things the children have put into their notes. For example, 'Dear...', or 'Thank you...', and their names. If you can, set up a post box in the classroom so the children can write notes to one another, and then post them.

Favourite kind of weather Have a short discussion about the range of different weather conditions that they could choose; hot and sunny, rainy, misty, frost and icy, snow and showery rain. Talk about the clothes that they might need to wear. When the diagrams come back, stick them in a 'favourite weather book'. You could write a short sentence to go with each picture so that the children can read it themselves.

Adverts Show the children a few real adverts for places (maybe holiday resorts, museums, or amusement parks) so that they have an idea of how to set theirs out. When the children bring back their adverts, display them around the class or school. Talk about which adverts are most eye-catching. What are the range of things that the children have chosen to advertise their school on the strength of?

Film events Have any of the children written about the same film as someone else? Have they even written about the same events? Do they agree about the order of events? Try re-writing the stories of their films using a storyboard method. Give the children sheets which have five or six boxes on them. The children have to write the story of their film in the boxes like a comic strip. The less able children can stick to just pictures; and the more able ones can fill in with speech bubbles.

Family and friends register Remind the children of the kinds of people they could include in their 'family' (distant cousins that they are great friends with, good friends of any kind friends of their parents, step-parents and siblings). When the children bring their lists back, you can use the names for data-handling work, and look for the most popular name. Display the children's pictures alongside a piece of writing explaining why these are their favourite people.

Favourite meal When the children bring back their 'plates' display them so that the children can all appreciate the range of different foods preferred by the children in the class. If there is an unusual meal spend some time discussing it. Who cooks the meal? How is it prepared? Invite a parent to come in and demonstrate how to make that food, and let all the children taste it.

Bedtime When the children bring back their bedtime routines, talk about how they all do things differently. At school, you could use the same idea with one of the daily routines in the school day; like 'tidy-up time', or going to assembly. You could make an instruction book for new children to refer to when they join the class.

Be careful! When the lists come back, talk about the range of dangers the children were aware of. Make up a whole class list. Use the list to write some 'safety first' rules for the kitchen. Are there any power points or hot water taps in your class? Perhaps the children could write warning signs for the classroom.

Firework safety When the lists come back, talk about the range of dangers the children were aware of. Make up a definitive whole class list. Use this list to write some 'safety first' rules for fireworks night. Make warning signs with the children that they can take home.

Animal babies Emphasise to the children that the purpose of this is to collect names of different animals and their babies and that these should be generic rather than affectionate (cat and kitten as opposed to Sooty and Miew Miew!). Display the children's pictures in a 'Family album' with a different animal with its young on each page.

Supercall Read out each message and then ask the children to guess which Superhero it comes from! Each child can paint a picture of their Superhero. Make a class book of Superhero messages and

impact WRITING HOMEWORK

Writing for a purpose

pictures. In class, the children can write a reply to their superhero and put that beside their original message.

My house Display the children's drawings. Discuss which parts of the building they labelled, and how the labels related to the picture. Did the labels go over parts of the picture or beside it? The children can now go outside and draw a picture of the school. Discuss which parts they could label. From their sketches, ask a group of children to produce one large painted picture of the school and then ask the other children to do neat labels for it.

Turn off the lights! Make a display of the children's signs. Discuss the reasons why we need to be careful to turn off the lights. Talk about saving energy and money! What other ways do we waste electricity? Can the children suggest some other areas of saving and make some new signs? Can they design a symbol which means 'turn off' just as we have a symbol which means 'don't smoke'?

Card of thanks! Show the children how to fold a piece of A4 paper in half and half again to make a card. Tell them that this size will fit the envelopes you will provide (6" x 4") to avoid a range of card sizes coming back! Back in school help write the recipient's name (and address if known) on the envelopes. Talk about how addresses are organised.

Fragile! Discuss how to sort and classify the different objects then discuss what the word unbreakable means. What things can the children think about which might have the label unbreakable on them? They can draw an unbreakable thing each and write the word underneath. Display both sets of pictures and labels into a class book. Use the heading 'Opposites: fragile and unbreakable' as a title.

Flower power Before this activity goes home, look at a copy of Van Gogh's *Sunflowers* and other works of art involving flowers. Discuss how the children could draw their flowers – in a very bold style or in a very delicate way. When the activity comes back, you can make a spectacular display of the children's pictures by encouraging them to paint a copy of the best flowers pictures. Don't forget that all the paintings need a title and a name plate! If any of the children don't have old cards to use at home, provide them with some spares from school.

Keep out! Before this activity goes home, show the children some examples of signs (for example the Highway Code). Talk about the type of symbol used and the shape of the sign (a red circle and a red triangle have specific meanings, for example). Discuss colours (red for danger!). When the activity comes back, the children can copy their sign on to a larger piece of paper and you can make a display of all the best signs.

TV postcard Supply the children with a plain white postcard each. When they bring back their postcards let each child read out their message. Can the others guess what programme the message refers to? Make a block graph of all the children's favourite programmes. They could each draw a picture of their favourite programme on a small rectangle of card, write their name on it and stick it in the appropriate column on the graph.

Wet paint! Before the activity goes home, look at a variety of signs. Discuss the sorts of images which they could use for their 'wet paint' signs. When the signs come back in, use them as the stimulus for creative writing. Ask the children to write a very short account of what happens when someone doesn't see a 'wet paint' sign. Read Jill Murphy's story *All in One Piece* (Walker) to the class.

Poison label Discuss with the children the different things that they think are poisonous and make a class list. Then, as a contrast, make a list together of all the things that are healthy to eat or drink. Make two displays – one of the poison labels with pictures of poisonous things and the other of the healthy things with labels attached saying 'eat me!' or 'drink me!'. The children can work in pairs drawing the pictures and labelling them clearly.

Certificate Show the children some different certificates before this goes home. Discuss what information needs to go on to the certificate: who is awarding the certificate; what it is for; who has received it; and who has authorised it. When the certificates come back in, the children can each write a short account of what they did to get their certificate! They can also draw a picture. Finally make a display of their certificates, their writing and their pictures, all together.

This way up Before this activity goes home, look at some examples of boxes with 'This way up' signs on them. Talk about how the arrow is used to show which way up. When the children's signs come back, construct some boxes, copy the signs on to them using paint, and display these. Make a list of the sorts of thing which have to be carried a certain way up. Did the children's suggestions include pets – or even people?

Medal Before this activity goes home, read the children the story of *Mog, the Forgetful Cat* by Judith Kerr (Picture Lions). When the children bring back their medals, encourage each child to write a short story about what they did to deserve their medal! They can illustrate their story. Make small books of all their stories – and paste their medals on to the front of each book. They can then take their books home to read to someone at home.

Picnic fare! Discuss the different lists that the children have brought in. Are there some items which are on all their lists? Are there some things which only one or two children like? Make a list for a class picnic. Perhaps you can organise to collect these things together and actually go on a picnic.

Stormy night! Before this activity goes home, bring in some examples of posters to show the children. Discuss what sorts of image they think they might want to put on their posters. When the children bring in their posters, share them all so that everyone can see them. Get the best ones copied by painting them on to larger sheets of paper.

Chewing string! The children can all discuss the sorts of thing which they are tempted to chew! (hair/collars of clothing/fingers!). They can each write a very short comic strip about a child who has got into the habit of chewing something and what happens to them. Before they do this writing, read them Hilaire Belloc's poem about Henry King (from Cautionary Verses (Random House)). Talk about what a cautionary tale is and how it works!

Animal caption Make a class book of all the pictures and captions. In class, they can choose either the same animal or a different one and write a three or four frame comic strip about that animal. The children can draw 'speech bubbles' for what their animal says in each frame. Mount their comic strips on the wall, with some large captions in speech bubbles for everyone to read.

Wake up! Discuss all the children's lists. Has everyone included the same things? Talk about which things you do every morning (like cleaning teeth!) and which things you do only sometime (like watching Breakfast TV or reading in bed).

Car of the year In school the children could produce painted versions of their cars and can label these. Some children might like to design a 'car of the future' and these can be labelled too.

impact WRITING HOMEWORK   **Writing for a purpose**   49

To the helper:

- Talk about the kind of thing you might have to record a message about. Perhaps you can make up a short story that provides the children with a setting for their telephone message.
- Remember, you do not need to write down every word of the message, just enough to let the other person understand what the message is.
- Help with any words your child gets stuck on.

The skill of writing comprehensible messages is an important one which will be needed in the future.

_____and
child

_____
helper(s)

_____
did this activity together

50   Writing for a purpose

Telephone message

Imagine that the phone rings, and you have to answer it.

The call is not for you, it is for someone else who lives in your house.

Who is calling and what do they say? (Perhaps someone has won a prize in a competition!)

● Write down the message in your writing.

impact WRITING HOMEWORK

PE lesson

- Write down one thing that we could do in PE next week. It could be Jump 5 times.

Write it very big so that everyone will be able to read it.

do 72 press-ups

do 100 sit-ups

do 25 vaults

do 60 jumps

impact WRITING HOMEWORK

To the helper:

- Talk about what your child does in PE.
- We are going to use these instructions as part of a real PE session, so the writing needs to be simple, big and clear.
- Help with the writing if necessary. You could use felt-tipped pens, crayons or paint.

This activity is a combination of an instruction-writing exercise, and sign-writing. Both skills encourage the children to communicate a message (or instruction), clearly and simply.

_____and
child

_____
helper(s)

_____
did this activity together

Writing for a purpose

To the helper:

- Talk about your child's favourite games. Can you remember any games that you enjoyed playing as a child? Are there any games that you used to play that are not played any more?
- You can take over with the writing if necessary.

List writing is an important skill that is very useful for collecting and sorting ideas.

_____ and
child

_____
helper(s)

did this activity together

Party games

Imagine that you are going to have a party.

What games would you like to play?

- Write a list.

52 **Writing for a purpose**

impact **WRITING HOMEWORK**

Breakfast shopping

Oh NO!

'The tiger who came to tea' has come for breakfast at your house and eaten everything...

● Can you write a shopping list to replace all the things that he ate?

impact WRITING HOMEWORK

To the helper:

● Talk about the story of *The Tiger who Came to Tea*. Can your child remember what happened? What did the tiger eat? What might he eat at your house?

● Talk about writing a shopping list; why do you need one?

Writing lists is an essential writing skill. It requires the children to sort and order their ideas. The purpose of this writing is to record a set of ideas that the children can then refer back to at a later date.

_____ and
child

_____
helper(s)

_____
did this activity together

Writing for a purpose 53

To the helper:

- Talk about the birthdays in your family. Which months are they in? Help your child with the spellings of the months. Talk about the sounds in the words; do they know all the letters?
- Whose birthdays come first, or last in the year?

We shall use everyone's birth dates at school to look more closely at the months in the year. Having to record this information in the form of writing gives the children a purpose for writing.

_____ and
child

_____
helper(s)

did this activity together

Writing for a purpose

Birthdays

When is your birthday?

● Write down the date.

Ask everyone in your home about their birthdays. See if you can write the date of their birthdays too.

Does anyone else have their birthday in the same month as you?

impact WRITING HOMEWORK

Favourite toys

Which are your favourite toys?

- Write a list of them. How many are there?
- Draw a picture of your favourite toy.

To the helper:

- Discuss which toys they like best and why. Help your child to write the list. They do not have to write every word – you can help by writing some!
- The list does not need to be very long – perhaps five or six toys. Discuss how to spell each toy.

We shall use the children's lists to make a graph of all the children's favourite toys. We shall also discuss how some of the toys can be described – and perhaps write some stories about our toys!

_____ and

child

_____

helper(s)

_____

did this activity together

impact WRITING HOMEWORK

Writing for a purpose 55

To the helper:

- Show your child how to break the task down into simple steps – for example 1 Take the toothbrush. 2 Run it under the tap. 3 Put the toothpaste on it and so on.
- We call it 'bossy language' because we use active verbs (imperatives) and short sharp sentences!

We shall compare the children's instructions. Do they always break the tasks down in the same way? Are all the steps the same? We shall be developing our writing skills by writing more complex sets of instructions in class.

_____ and

child

_____

helper(s)

_____

did this activity together

Bossy language!

Use 'bossy language' to tell someone how to do something!

- Write a list of instructions. It needs to be something very simple like cleaning your teeth or washing your face! Each instruction must be clear and easy to follow.

Writing for a purpose

impact WRITING HOMEWORK

ID card

Make an identity card for yourself.

You will need to include:

- a picture of yourself
- your name
- your height (in centimetres)
- the colour of your eyes

Name _____
Height _____
Colour of eyes _____

To the helper:

- Do you have any ID cards? If so have a look at how they are set out, and the kind of information that is on them.
- Help your child find out the information that is needed for the card, and with the writing if needed. Do you have a suitable photograph which can be stuck onto the sheet?

Making an ID card provides the children with a format for writing down specific items of information about themselves. We shall be talking about the ID cards at school.

_____ and
child

_____
helper(s)

_____
did this activity together

impact WRITING HOMEWORK

Writing for a purpose 57

To the helper:

- You might need help to jog your child's memory! Perhaps together you will be able to think of something.
- This does not have to be a proper letter, just a note. Let your child do what they can, and you do whatever else is needed.

Writing letters and notes are important forms of writing with which the children need to be familiar. We shall discuss how the children got on with their writing at school.

_____and

child

_____

helper(s)

_____

did this activity together

Thank you note

Can you think of something nice that has happened to you recently?

Who was involved? Was it your Mum, Dad, sister, brother, best friend...?

- Write a short letter to them saying 'Thank you'. Bring the letter to school before you send it.

Favourite kind of weather

What is your favourite weather? Sunny or snowy?

What clothes would you need to wear to play outside in your favourite kind of weather?

- Draw a picture of you ready to play.
- Label three things which you are wearing.

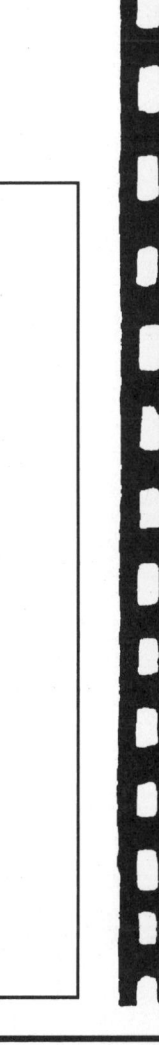

To the helper:

- Talk about your child's favourite weather. What is it? What games can you play when it is like that? What kind of clothes would they need to wear?
- Help with the labelling if needed. You could draw the first line from the item of clothing you are going to label, and your child could do the rest once they have the idea.

Labelling is an important purpose for writing. We shall be discussing the children's diagrams at school, and the different weather conditions that they prefer.

_____and

child

_____

helper(s)

_____

did this activity together

impact WRITING HOMEWORK

Writing for a purpose 59

To the helper:

- Talk about the kind of thing that would be good to put on an advert. For example: how friendly the children are, how much fun you can have in the class, or in the playground.
- Help with writing the slogans around the picture if needed.

Writing adverts is one form of writing for a purpose. A certain message has to be communicated clearly, and attractively. We shall display the children's 'adverts' at school.

_____and
child

_____
helper(s)

did this activity together

60 **Writing for a purpose**

Adverts

Design an advert for your school.

● Draw a picture, and write a few words that say something good about it.

impact WRITING HOMEWORK

Film events

Think of a film you have seen recently on TV or at the cinema.

- Write down three things that happened in the order in which they happened.
- Draw pictures to go with each one.

To the helper:

- Talk about the most recent film your child has seen. Can they tell you the plot? Emphasise keeping the events in the correct order.
- Pick three things that you could write down, and then draw illustrations for.

Recording events that happened in the plot of a film provides the children with a purpose for writing. We shall discuss the films that the children have seen at school, and consider their storylines.

_____and
child

_____
helper(s)

_____

did this activity together

impact WRITING HOMEWORK

Writing for a purpose 61

To the helper:

- Talk about your immediate family, and your extended family and friends who are important to your child.
- Help with the spellings of the different names.

Writing lists is an important skill that the children will use frequently in the future. We shall be talking about the children's 'Special people' back at school.

_____ and
child

_____
helper(s)

did this activity together

Family and friends register

Who do you consider to be a part of your family? Would you include close family friends or neighbours?

● Write a list of all the people who are in your family, and others who you would consider as 'family'. Find out how to spell their names.

☆ Family and friends register ☆   ☆ Family and friends register ☆

62 **Writing for a purpose**

impact WRITING HOMEWORK

Favourite meal

What is your favourite meal?

● Draw it on this plate, and write down what it is.

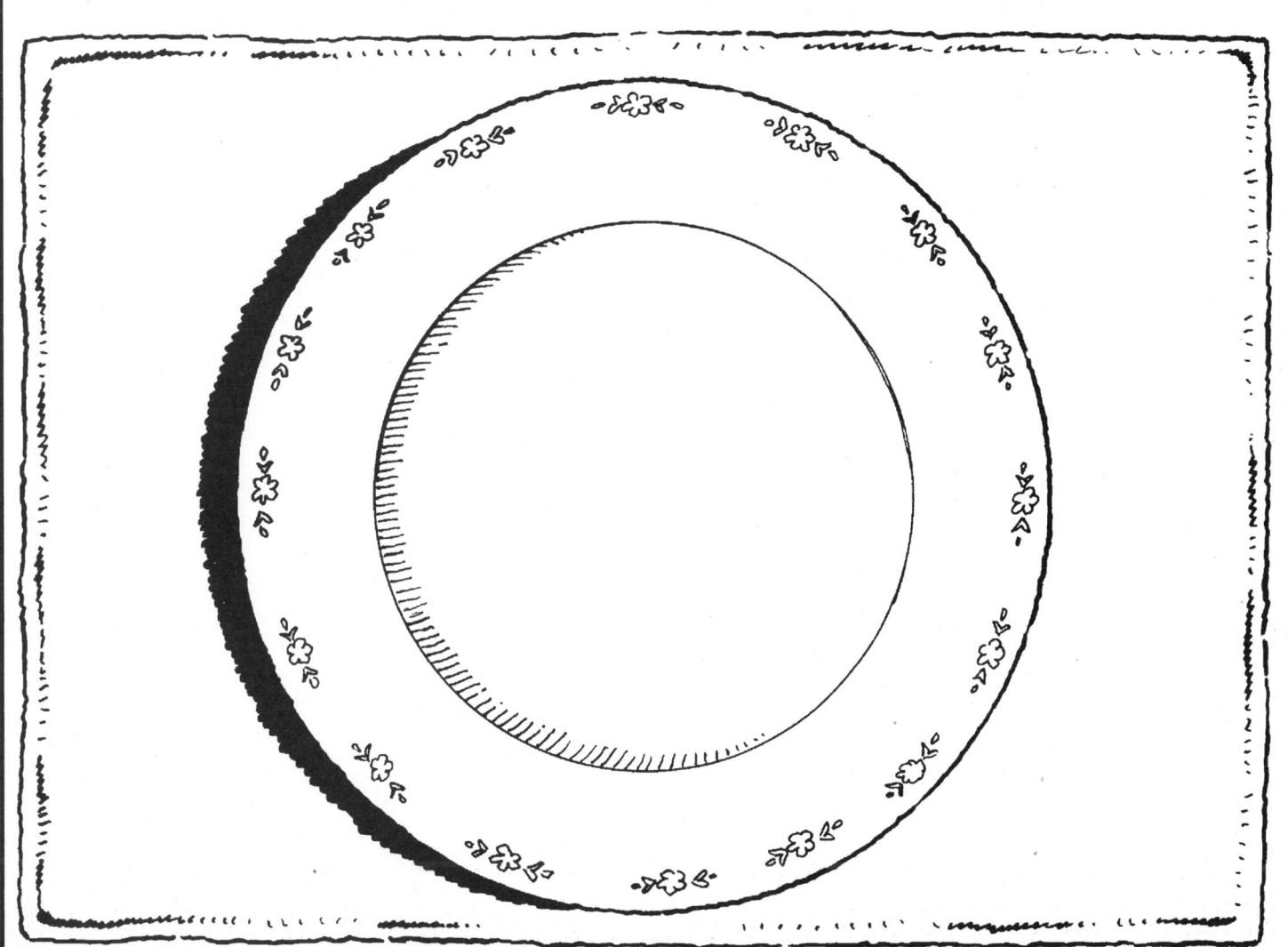

To the helper:
● What foods does your child like to eat the most? Are they healthy or unhealthy?
● Help with the writing if needed.

Recording information is an important purpose for writing. We shall talk about all the children's favourite meals at school.

_____and
child

_____
helper(s)

_____
did this activity together

impact WRITING HOMEWORK

Writing for a purpose   63

To the helper:

● Talk through your child's bedtime routine, if they have one. For example, does your child have a story read to them, have a last drink, brush their teeth?
● Help with the writing if necessary.

Writing out their bedtime routine in the correct order gives a purpose for writing, and will help develop ordering skills, which in turn will help with storytelling skills.

_____ and
child

_____
helper(s)

did this activity together

Bedtime

How do you get ready for bed each night?

● Draw three pictures showing the things you do to get ready for bed in the order that you do them in.

Write what you are doing in each picture.

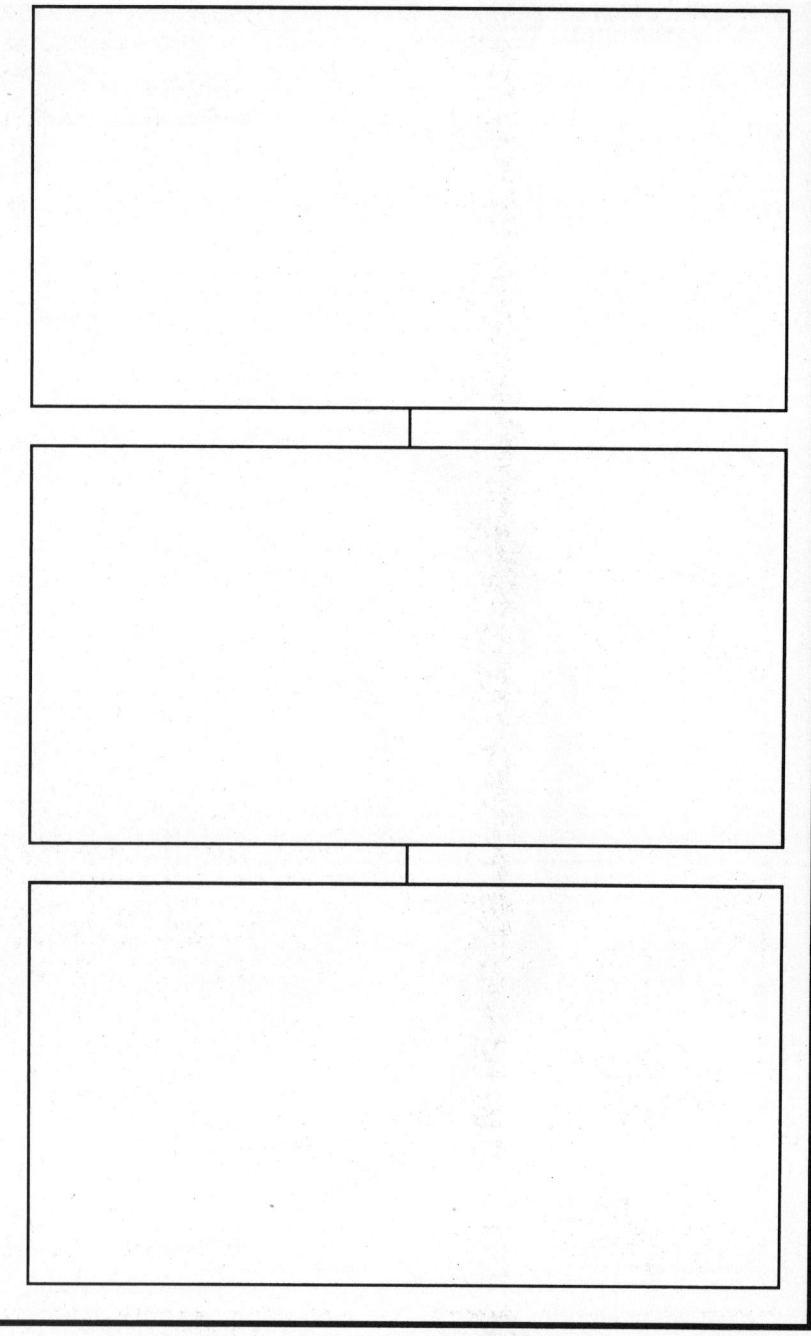

64 **Writing for a purpose**

impact WRITING HOMEWORK

Be careful!

- Write down five things you must be careful of in the kitchen.

Use pictures to illustrate your list.

To the helper:

- Have a look together in the kitchen to see which places might be dangerous (especially to children).
- Help with writing down the list if needed.

Writing lists is an important skill which will be useful to the children in several areas of their life in the future. We shall discuss the places/things they considered dangerous in the class.

_____and
child

_____
helper(s)

did this activity together

impact WRITING HOMEWORK

Writing for a purpose 65

To the helper:

- Talk about the dangers of firework night. Discuss potential dangers of bonfires and fireworks if they are used incorrectly.

Writing lists is an important skill which will be useful to the children in several areas of their life in the future. We shall discuss the places/things they considered dangerous in class.

_____ and
child

_____
helper(s)

did this activity together

66   **Writing for a purpose**

Firework safety

- Write down five things that you must be careful of on firework night.

Use pictures to illustrate the list.

impact WRITING HOMEWORK

Animal babies

Do you know what baby animals are called?

- Choose an animal and draw it with its baby. Write down their proper names.

To the helper:

- Talk through which animals you both like. Do you have any pets?

Finding out what certain animal babies are called provides the children with a purpose for writing. We shall be talking about all the different animals that the children thought of at school.

_____ and
child

_____
helper(s)

_____
did this activity together

impact WRITING HOMEWORK

Writing for a purpose 67

To the helper:

- Talk about which Superhero your child might like to get a telephone call from. Remember 'hero' can include 'heroines'!
- Help write the message down – it doesn't need to be very long.

Writing messages provides an excellent purpose for having to put pen to paper – particularly if children find the actual writing process quite hard.

_____ and

child

_____

helper(s)

_____

did this activity together

Supercall

Imagine that you have just had a telephone call.

A Superhero has phoned you up and given you an important message to pass on.

What was the message?

- Write it down.

Writing for a purpose

impact WRITING HOMEWORK

My house

- Draw a picture of the building where you live. (You will need to go outside to look at it.)

On which floor do you live?

Where is your bedroom?

How many windows are there altogether?

- Label your drawing.

To the helper:

- Go outside together to look at the building. How many floors are there? Which floor do you live on? Discuss how they will draw the building. What shape is it? How many windows can you see?
- When they have completed their drawing, help them to label one or two aspects of it, for example their own bedroom window.

Labelling drawings and diagrams is an obvious use of writing and helps children to see that the written word is very useful, even on a picture!

_____ and
child

_____
helper(s)

_____
did this activity together

impact WRITING HOMEWORK

Writing for a purpose 69

To the helper:

● What will the sign need to say? What picture might it have? Discuss the words which may go on the sign with your child, and perhaps write them down first. Discuss the picture – what images are a good idea?

Signs are an important means of communication. The children will need to think about the purpose of their words – and the images that accompany it.

_____ and

child

_____

helper(s)

_____

did this activity together

70 **Writing for a purpose**

Turn off the lights!

Leaving lights on wastes electricity and costs money!

● Make a sign to remind people in your home to turn off the lights!

impact WRITING HOMEWORK

Card of thanks!

- Make a 'Thank you' card for someone who has done something nice for you recently. It should be someone outside your family – a friend or a neighbour, perhaps a teacher!

- Design the front of the card, and draw a really good picture to go on it.

- Write a message inside.

To the helper:

- Talk about who the child could make a card for. Has anyone taken them out, or given them a present? It would be nice to make the picture on the front of the card personal, for example a drawing of the outing or gift. Talk about the message. The card can just say 'Thank you' or it can have a longer message.

Cards provide a useful purpose for writing – and drawing! We shall look at the cards back in the class, and then we shall put them in envelopes ready to be sent.

_____and

child

_____

helper(s)

_____

did this activity together

impact WRITING HOMEWORK

Writing for a purpose 71

To the helper:

- Talk to your child about the things in your home which are fragile. Which do you value most? Why?

Notices and signs provide a real-life purpose for writing. We shall discuss all their signs back in class and make a lovely display of the children's work.

_____ and
child

_____
helper(s)

_____
did this activity together

72   **Writing for a purpose**

Fragile!

● Draw a picture of something in your home which you have to handle with great care! Write fragile across the bottom.

impact WRITING HOMEWORK

Flower power

Imagine you are going to send someone some flowers. Think who you would like to send them to.

- Draw the bunch of flowers you would like to send.
- Write a message to go with the flowers here.

To the helper:
- Discuss who they would most like to send flowers to. Talk about what kind they would like to send – a plant pot, white flowers, yellow flowers, roses or leaves. Then discuss what they should write for their message. Use the back of an old birthday card to make a small card with the finished message on.

Writing cards – especially those which require just a few words – provides an excellent context for small children to write. We shall look at their drawings and cards in the classroom and make a display.

_____ and
child

_____
helper(s)

_____
did this activity together

Writing for a purpose

To the helper:

- Talk about where your child would hang their notice – perhaps on their bedroom door! Perhaps on a desk or drawer or toybox! Discuss the words on the notice, and what picture should be drawn.

Signs and notices provide an excellent purpose for children's writing. We shall display all their notices and talk about what they want to protect.

_____ and
child

_____
helper(s)

did this activity together

74   **Writing for a purpose**

Keep out!

- Design a notice which tells everyone to 'Keep out'!

Where would you hang it? Write down where.

impact WRITING HOMEWORK

TV postcard

- Write a postcard to the producer of your favourite TV programme.
- Draw a picture on the front.
- Write a message on the back.

To the helper:

- Talk to your child about which is their favourite TV programme. What will they draw? What would they like to say to the people who make the programme?

Letters and postcards provide a real-life purpose for writing. Children are encouraged to see that they – like adults – can really communicate using the written word. We shall look at all their postcards and then send them to the TV producers they are addressed to.

_____ and
child

_____
helper(s)

_____
did this activity together

impact WRITING HOMEWORK

Writing for a purpose

To the helper:

• Have you seen signs alerting people to wet paint? Where have you seen these? Discuss how the sign can be made most effective?

Signs and posters provide a good reason for mixing images and words. The children can relate what they draw to what they write, and they do not have to write too much! We shall make a classroom display of all their posters and signs in the classroom.

_____and
child

_____
helper(s)

_____
did this activity together

76 **Writing for a purpose**

Wet paint!

• Design a poster to warn people that there is wet paint!

What picture will you draw to show people not to touch the wet paint? What words will you need to use?

impact WRITING HOMEWORK

Poison label

Some things are very bad for you if you eat or drink them!

- Make a 'Beware, Poison!' label.

Think what to put on the label. What will you draw? What words will you write?

To the helper:

- Talk about which things are poisonous. Discuss how dangerous some of these things are. What pictures and words can be used to show this?

Signs and posters provide a good reason for using images and words together. The children can relate what they draw to what they write – and they do not have to write too much! We shall make a display of all their posters and signs in the classroom.

_____and
child

_____
helper(s)

_____
did this activity together

impact WRITING HOMEWORK

Writing for a purpose 77

To the helper:

- Talk about how the certificate should look and what information it must have, for example what it is for, who it is to, who has awarded it, the date and so on. Talk about how it should be decorated to make it look grand.

This gives children a reason for producing clear writing in a certain style. We shall share our certificates in school and discuss the different things they have been awarded for!

_____ and
child

_____
helper(s)

did this activity together

Writing for a purpose

Certificate

Award yourself a certificate for something that you do well every day. It could be brushing your teeth! Or washing your face! Or even keeping your room tidy!

- Make the certificate using words and pictures and write your name on it!

This certificate is awarded for

Date:-

Anne Patterson

This way up

Is there something in your house that must be placed a certain way up?

- Make a label for it, saying which way up it should go.

To the helper:

- Have you seen signs telling people which way up a box must be carried? Discuss how the sign can be most effective.

Signs provide a good reason for writing. The children can make a sign which communicates clearly using words and images. We shall use their signs for a display in the classroom.

_____ and
child

_____
helper(s)

_____
did this activity together

impact WRITING HOMEWORK

Writing for a purpose 79

To the helper:

- Talk to your child about an occasion when they were brave. It does not need to be very grand! It could have been when they were lost, or fell over.
- Talk about how they will draw their picture inside a circle. Help them to write their name around the edge.

These medals will provide the stimulus for a discussion about things which have happened to us. The children will do some more writing based on these experiences in the classroom.

_____and
child

_____
helper(s)

_____
did this activity together

80 **Writing for a purpose**

Medal

Have you ever done something brave?

Give yourself a medal!

- Draw a picture of what happened in this circle.
- Write your name around the edge.

impact WRITING HOMEWORK

Picnic fare!

- Make a list here of all the things that you would like to take to eat and drink on a picnic.

- Draw a picture of your favourite item here.

To the helper:

- Talk to your child about picnics. Point out that the food has to be carried, so it shouldn't need to be kept hot or very cold for example.

Lists provide a real-life context in which children see adults writing. We shall collect their ideas together to make one large exciting picnic list in the classroom.

_____ and

child

_____

helper(s)

_____

did this activity together

impact WRITING HOMEWORK

Writing for a purpose 81

To the helper:

- Talk to your child about storms and about the sorts of work which go on at night and might be affected by storms. (Fishermen, the police, nurses, bus and train drivers, aeroplane pilots and factory workers).
- Discuss where you might display their poster.

Signs and posters provide an excellent purpose for writing. Communicating clearly through both words and images is an important skill. We shall use the children's posters for a display in class.

_____ and
child

_____
helper(s)

did this activity together

82 **Writing for a purpose**

Stormy night!

Imagine the weather forecast is for a stormy night with lots of rain, wind and thunderstorms.

You have to design a warning poster for people who have to go out tonight!

- Draw a good picture and write a few words to warn people that storms are on their way.

impact WRITING HOMEWORK

Chewing string!

'The chief defect of Henry King
Was chewing little bits of string!' (Hilaire Belloc)

Do you, or does anyone else in your family, put things in their mouth and chew them? Some toddlers chew a blanket or a sheet, and lots of people chew their pencil!

- Make a sign warning people about putting things which are not food in their mouth!

To the helper:

- Talk to your child about babies and toddlers and how important it is for them to 'taste' things. Discuss the things which are safe to chew, and those which are dangerous.
- Help your child to design a sign, once they have decided who it is aimed at!

Signs and posters provide an excellent purpose for writing. Most children will remember enjoying chewing or sucking things when they were younger. We shall use their signs as a stimulus for more discussion and writing in class.

_____ and
child

_____
helper(s)

_____

did this activity together

impact WRITING HOMEWORK

Writing for a purpose 83

To the helper:

- Help your child find a picture. It could be a photo of a family pet, or it could be cut out of a magazine or comic. Talk to your child about the picture. Help them to think of something funny that the animal might be saying.

Writing dialogue is quite a difficult skill. Starting by thinking of a caption is quite a good means of introducing this. We shall use all the captions in school to stimulate some more writing in dialogue.

_____and
child

_____
helper(s)

_____
did this activity together

84   **Writing for a purpose**

Animal caption

Find a picture of a pet or an animal.
What does the animal look as if it might be saying?

- Write a caption for the picture.

Next time, can you please not throw it so far!

impact WRITING HOMEWORK

Wake up!

How do you get up in the morning? Do you always do things in the same order?

- Write a list of the things you do when you wake up.
- Draw a picture of your favourite part of your 'wake up' list!

To the helper:

- Help your child by talking through the sequence of events in the morning. Do they get dressed straight away or eat breakfast in their pyjamas. Help them to list what happens in order.

Making lists is an essential writing skill. Children see adults making and using lists. This activity helps them to start ordering their thoughts and experiences in list form.

_____ and
child

_____
helper(s)

_____
did this activity together

impact WRITING HOMEWORK

Writing for a purpose   85

To the helper:

- Help choose the car and discuss the shape and colour.
- Discuss the various parts which all cars need, for example wheels, steering wheel or windscreen. Choose three or four obvious parts for them to label.

Labelling a drawing or diagram provides a useful reason for writing, especially at this age when writing just a few words can be an effort. We shall make a list of all the labelled parts in class.

_____ and
child

_____
helper(s)

did this activity together

86 **Writing for a purpose**

Name:-   Date:

Car of the year

What is your favourite car?

- Draw a picture of it and label the parts.

impact WRITING HOMEWORK

Teachers' Notes
YEAR TWO

Fantasy holiday Bring some travel brochures in to show the children before the activity goes home. When the children bring back their posters, talk about the most eye-catching points. What kind of detail have they thought of? Who is their poster for? Make a corner of the classroom into a travel agents and display the posters.

Bookmark When the children bring back their bookmarks get them to talk to the other children about which book their bookmark goes with. Which words have they written on their bookmark; does it give away the story, or does it just get you interested? Display the bookmarks near the book corner where all the children can see them.

Rubbish and more rubbish! Before this activity goes home, go through a selection of rubbish that has been thrown out from the classroom that day. How much of it is recyclable? Does your school recycle anything? Talk about the kinds of material that can be recycled. When the posters come back, talk about how effective some of the children's methods are at making them eye-catching.

Traffic signs This activity would fit in with any work you are doing about safety in the home *or* traffic signs. Talk about how different kinds of traffic signs are different shapes, and how the shape itself gives a message. Traffic signs actually have very few words on them, maybe one or two, with most of the message being communicated through a picture. Explain that they will have to think very carefully about their choice of words, since they will be using so few! When the children bring back their signs, see if the other children can guess where the sign is meant to be displayed, and what it is warning us about.

Golden oldies Start the activity off by bringing in one of your own oldest toys. Either before or after this activity read *Old Bear* by Jane Hissey (Red Fox), or *Midnight Teddies* by Dana Kubrick (Walker) together. When the children bring back their memories, get a few of them to read some of their writing out loud to the class. You could sort the toys into types or order the toys by the age of the children when they were given the toy. Write stories about the toys.

Party invitation Before this activity goes home, show the children a few examples of party invitations with tear-off strips on them. What kind of information are you given and asked for? When the children bring back their invitations, look at the information: will people know where to come, which day and time to come, and who the invitation is from? Would the tear-off strip give enough information about the person replying?

Ooh it's so irritating! Display the children's posters around the class, and talk about the kinds of things they would like to ban people from doing in the class, or in public places. Have they used symbols to denote 'no' such as crosses, or the sign used in roadsigns (the red circle with a line across it)?

Crazy crazes! Before the activity goes home, talk to the children about what sort of thing might be considered a craze. For example marbles, Pogs, Teenage Mutant Ninja Turtles or Football cards. When the children bring back their writing, talk about the crazes they have identified. Do adults have fads or is it only children?

Ice cream compendium Talk about the range of flavours the children have thought of. Where did they get their ideas? Make a compilation list of all the flavours. Sort the ice creams: into alphabetical order/colour /flavour groups? Ask the children to describe their favourite flavours using as many adjectives as they can in one sentence.

Pet care Talk about the animals that the children thought of, and the care that they need. Perhaps you have a pet in your classroom? Discuss the dangers of 'overcare', for example overfeeding, watering and grooming, which can happen in a classroom situation. Invite someone in to talk to the class: a vet or someone who works at a local park or animal hospital.

Dial 999 Compare the children's instructions. Did some people leave something out? Did anyone put in an unnecessary line? Compile a class list of instructions and pin them on the wall. Ask the children what the circumstances are in which you might need to dial 999. The children can write a short story about an emergency where they have to dial 999.

A place for everything… How tidy are the children in your class? Discuss the different places we put things in the classroom. Make a 'Tidy-Book' with a list of objects drawn opposite the places they have to be put away. Make labels to go on things to help them remember. Let the children each make a label for something at home and let them take it home!

Telephone call How have the children set out their instructions? Are they clear and easy to follow? Read out a few of the sets of instructions, and get another child to follow them word-for-word. Does it depend what kind of phone you are using, or who you are calling? Ask the children to make up and write a few imaginary phone calls. Give them a range of different situations to choose from.

Saturday mornings List all the Saturday morning occupations. How many children do each activity. Are there some activities that only one or two children engage in? Make a graph of their Saturday morning occupations. Perhaps the children can write a short paragraph each, describing their favourite Saturday morning.

Favourite books / Television favourites / Review What type of books/television programmes/films are the most popular? Make a class list of favourite titles. Investigate the most popular genres: do boys generally like one genre, and girls another? Why is this? Ask the children to talk about their favourites in turn, and say what they particularly enjoyed about them. Ask one child each week to choose their favourite, and to explain it to the other children, and describe why they would recommend it to others.

Meal ratings When the children bring back their menus display them so that all the children can appreciate the range of different foods that the children like. If a child does write down something which is unfamiliar to the rest of the class spend some time discussing that meal. Who cooks the meal? How do they prepare it? If you can arrange it, ask a parent to demonstrate the meal. Let all the children taste it.

Favourite games Which types of games are the most popular? Make a class list. Investigate the most popular genres of game. Do boys generally like one genre of game, and girls another?

Top toy Show the children some real adverts for toys (such as in magazines), so that the children have an idea of how to set their's out. The children can discuss their favourite toys. Do some children share favourites? Encourage the children to describe their toys. Make a list of all their descriptive words. They could write stories about their toys, or descriptions to go with their drawings.

Be safe! When the children bring back their diagrams, discuss the range of different clothes they have chosen. There is a slogan on posters: 'Children should be seen and not hurt'. Talk about what this means and why it is clever. Can the children think up any more slogans that people might remember? Display the posters around the school.

Crossing the road Compile a comprehensive, concise class list of all the ideas. The children can then use this list to make posters to display around the school. Invite a police officer, or a lollipop person in to talk about road safety. Although it is important for children to learn how to cross a road safely at this age, remember that children under eight or nine years old should not be crossing busy roads as they are not sufficiently developed in all their senses (perception of traffic speed etc).

Ha ha ha! Remind the children that their helper can help write the joke down if necessary. Tell a few of the jokes each day and then put them in to a class joke book which the children can read to one another. These can also be quite useful as fillers for a school magazine or booklet!

Save water! Before the children take this activity home, look at some examples of posters together. Talk about what images could be used, and how slogans should not use too many words. When their posters come in, the children can improve and enlarge them by painting them onto larger pieces of paper. Have a class brainstorm and make a list of all the ways in which we could save water. Talk about re-using water, and the use of rainwater. Perhaps the children can design ways to catch rainwater where they live, for example on window sills, or off the roof?

More please! Make a class list, drawing on all the best reasons which the children have come up with. Discuss how much pocket money the children can agree is reasonable for a person of six or seven years old. Can the children think of reasons why it might be bad to have too much pocket money?

Cat collar Talk about the minimum information that is necessary to make sure that the cat can be delivered back home if lost. Why might it be a bad idea to include the cat's name? The children can use this activity to write a short story about a cat who gets lost. Read *The Patchwork Cat* by Nicola Bayley (Red Fox) first and let the children work in pairs to plan their stories.

Luggage label Discuss how we write our name and address. Talk about the layout – and the order. Do the children all know their postcodes? Use the children's ideas about holiday destinations for creative writing.

Excuses, excuses Collect in all the excuses and read them out in turn. Ask the children to guess who wrote each one! Which excuses are most plausible? Which are the funniest? Read *John Patrick Norman McHennessey* by John Burningham (Beaver Books) and put the children in groups to write their own version. They can each do one double spread, with a different excuse on each one, which can be illustrated. Put all the pages together to make a lovely book called 'Excuses, excuses!'.

Can't go now! The children can choose the best excuses and write them out neatly on some large sheets of paper. Discuss what time is a reasonable bedtime. Ask whether you might ever want to go to bed early! Ask the children to write a short account of a time when they went to bed very late – perhaps they were coming back from a journey or it was a special occasion!

There's a frog in my porridge! When all the notes come in, read each one out in turn to the class. Can the children guess who wrote each one! Talk about the things that the children like to eat and the things that they do not like! Do some children like things that other children hate? The children can draw pictures of their favourite meal, and then write a list of all the ingredients.

Welcome here Before this activity goes home, bring in some posters for the children to look at. Talk about the fact that there will need to be some images as well as some words on this 'welcome' poster. When the children bring in their posters, make a display – perhaps in the entrance hall of the school. Talk to the children about the reasons why we come to school. Make a list of all the reasons we can think of! Which ones are most important? Which ones are least important?

Silence Share all the children's signs. Which ones do they think are particularly good and why? Make an agreed list of all the places where it is important to 'be quiet'! Now discuss making a noise. Why is it important to have places where children – and grown-ups can shout? Can the children think of places where groups of children or adults do shout? (Playgrounds or football grounds for example.)

No free newspapers Before this activity goes home, let the children look at some examples of signs. The Highway Code is useful in this context. Talk about what images can be used and what shape the sign might be (circle and triangle road signs mean different things!). Discuss the use of colour (red for danger!). Discuss why we might not want/want free newspapers. Make a list of the reasons for and against free newspapers. Have a class discussion.

Shoes off! Talk about the children's signs. Who has come up with the best image? Who has got the message across most succinctly? Discuss other things which you are often being told off about at home – perhaps making too much noise or mess, or rushing about too wildly, or quarrelling!

Ladies and gentlemen Look at examples of 'Ladies' and 'Gentlemen' signs. Make a class collection of as many different types as you can find. Encourage them to find out the words for 'Ladies' and 'Gentlemen' in other languages. How can they make the signs clear and also attractive? The best signs could be copied onto card and laminated to be put on the actual school toilet doors!

A wish, please! The children can read out their wishes to one another. Have any children chosen the same wish? Let a group of children paint a *large* picture of the genie and then ask them to write out their wishes on coloured pieces of paper cut in the shape of bubbles. Display all the wish bubbles around the genie paintings.

Wake-up words Read out some of the children's ideas. Talk about how people can be woken gently, and how they can be woken roughly! The children can work in pairs to plan a short comic strip about what happens if they get woken up suddenly one day! They can make it as funny as they like. Make a display entitled 'waking up' which has both the comic strips and the 'wake-up words'.

Good-night all When the children's 'good-night words' come back in, select some of them to read to the whole class. Talk about the tactics the children themselves use to 'put off' bedtime. The children can write a short story, where they manage to postpone bedtime. Let them illustrate it – some words and a painting or drawing on each page.

Farewell my lovely Compile a class list of all the different forms of transport that anyone has mentioned. Make a tally chart to show how many times each one was mentioned. Put the children in groups to paint each form of transport. Look at the globe. Discuss in which areas of the world each different form of transport might be appropriate.

Fantasy holiday

Where would you most like to go on holiday?

Why would you choose that place?

- Design a poster showing all the wonderful things about that place.

Make sure that you write the name of the place on your poster.

To the helper:

- Talk about places you have been or would like to go on holiday. Try and find out about the place, or imagine all the wonderful things.
- Who is the poster for? Is it to attract adults, or other children? What things might attract them?
- If you can get hold of them, travel brochures are free, and might give you some more ideas.

Making posters is one type of writing for a purpose. Information has to be communicated in an eye-catching and clear way. We shall display and talk about the posters at school.

_____and
child

_____
helper(s)

did this activity together

impact WRITING HOMEWORK

Writing for a purpose 89

To the helper:

- Talk about the book your child is reading at the moment. What is it about? What kind of book is it?
- What words could your child write on the bookmark: the title; some hints about the plot; the character names?

Making a bookmark about a specific book provides the children with an interesting context.

_____ and
child

_____
helper(s)

_____
did this activity together

Bookmark

● Design a bookmark to use in the book you are reading at the moment.

Make it bright and colourful, and use ideas from the book to illustrate and write on it.

(Don't forget to write your name on it too.)

90 **Writing for a purpose**

impact WRITING HOMEWORK

Rubbish and more rubbish!

● Make a poster that encourages people to recycle their rubbish. Distinguish between the different kinds of rubbish that gets thrown away at your house.

For example:

- paper
- plastic
- cans
- glass

If you want, you could brighten up your poster with labels, or words cut from rubbish at home!

To the helper:

● Do you recycle any of your rubbish, or sort your rubbish at all? Talk about how different kinds of rubbish can be recycled.

● What kinds of words might you have on your poster? How will you grab people's attention?

Making posters is one type of writing for a purpose. Information has to be communicated in an attractive eye-catching and clear way. We shall display and talk about the posters at school.

_____ and
child

_____
helper(s)

did this activity together

impact WRITING HOMEWORK

Writing for a purpose   91

To the helper:

- Talk about the potential dangers in, for example, a kitchen. Have a look around; where are the power points? What fire risks are there? What about the bathroom?

Writing signs will help children be clear and concise about what they write. It helps them to learn to use precise language.

_____ and
child
_____
helper(s)
_____
did this activity together

Traffic signs

- Design a sign that will warn people about a dangerous place in the home. Make it like a traffic sign – you could put it near a cooker or a fire for example.

What shape are warning signs?

92 **Writing for a purpose**

impact WRITING HOMEWORK

Golden oldies

- Write what you can remember about your oldest toy.
- You could draw a picture of your toy too.

Which is your oldest toy?

When did you get it?

How old were you?

Who gave it to you?

To the helper:

- This might mean a lot of writing; if your child can remember a lot of things! Perhaps you could take over when your child gets tired.

This activity demonstrates a way of writing for a purpose; that is that their memories can now be shared by anyone else who can read. Back at school, the children will be able to share their memories, and some will be able to read theirs to the class.

_____ and
child

_____
helper(s)

_____
did this activity together

impact WRITING HOMEWORK

Writing for a purpose 93

To the helper:

- Talk about all the things that need to be on an invitation.
- Help with the writing if necessary.

This activity will help the children focus on one of the ways in which writing is important and useful in real life.

_____and
child

_____
helper(s)

_____
did this activity together

Party invitation

Pretend you are going to have a party.

- Design a party invitation that shows when and where the party is, with a tear-off reply strip at the bottom.

You could use pictures too.

94 Writing for a purpose

impact WRITING HOMEWORK

Ooh it's so irritating!

Is there something that people do which really annoys you?

Imagine that you can design and display a poster banning people from doing this thing.

Your poster could be for school, the bus, or any public place.

- Bring your poster to school.

To the helper:

- Talk about the kinds of things that really annoy you that other people do: listening to personal stereos (but you can still hear it); leaving chewing gum on the floor/on furniture; snoring and many others!

Writing signs and posters will help the children be clear and consise about what they write. It helps them to learn to use precise language, and to communicate a message clearly.

_____ and
child

_____
helper(s)

_____
did this activity together

impact WRITING HOMEWORK

Writing for a purpose 95

To the helper:

- Children of this age seem to be constantly coming in and out of crazes initated either by toy manufacturers, or the film and television industry. What things has your child been desperate to have, that everyone else has?

This activity makes the children think about, and identify a craze that they either observed, or were involved in. These are 'fads' that really capture the children's imagination. We shall use this for further writing work at school.

_____and
child

_____
helper(s)

_____
did this activity together

Crazy crazes!

Has there ever been a craze for something in your class or school?

● Write down what the craze was, and what you needed to have to be included in the craze.

96 **Writing for a purpose**

impact WRITING HOMEWORK

Ice-cream compendium

How many ice-cream flavours can you think of.

- Write a list.

- What is **your** favourite flavour?

To the helper:

- Talk about all the flavours you can think of. Give a hand writing down any of the more difficult ones.

Writing lists is an important skill which will be useful to the children in the future. We shall use the lists of ice-cream flavours in school.

_____ and
child

_____
helper(s)

_____
did this activity together

impact WRITING HOMEWORK

Writing for a purpose   97

To the helper:

● Talk about pets you know of. Choose one to think about. What do you think they need? (For example; food, water, toys, taking for walks and so on.)

Writing lists is an important skill which will be useful to the children in several areas of their life in the future. We shall use the list of things that the children thought of in the classroom.

_____ and
child
_____
helper(s)
_____
did this activity together

98 **Writing for a purpose**

Pet care

Do you have a pet? Or do you know someone with a pet?

● Write down three things you would need to take care of it.

impact WRITING HOMEWORK

Dial 999

How do you make an emergency call?

Talk to your helper about how to do this.

- Write a series of instructions to tell someone else how to do this.

To the helper:

- Talk to your child about the sort of circumstances in which a 999 call is required. Discuss how the call is actually made, and which service would be required.

Writing accurate instructions is one of the hardest skills to acquire. It is not until children – and adults have practised a great deal that they become proficient at this!

_____and
child

_____
helper(s)

_____

did this activity together

impact WRITING HOMEWORK

Writing for a purpose

To the helper:

● This is a good opportunity to talk about where things go. Does your child know where to put things away?

Writing lists is an important skill which will be useful to the children in the future. We shall use these lists of things that the children thought of at school, to talk about where things go in the classroom.

_____and
child

_____
helper(s)

did this activity together

100   **Writing for a purpose**

A place for everything...

Where does everything belong in your house?

● Write down five things which you use, and the names of the places where you put them away.

impact WRITING HOMEWORK

Telephone call

Do you know how to make a telephone call?

- Write down five instructions to help someone make a call.

To the helper:

- It might help to actually make a telephone call with your child. Ask your child to give you instructions on what to do.
- Try writing the instructions down in the correct order.

Writing instructions requires the children to organise their thoughts clearly, so that another person will understand what they must do.

_____and
child

_____
helper(s)

_____
did this activity together

Writing for a purpose 101

To the helper:

● Talk about your child's hobbies. Do they watch TV, or do they go out and do something? Perhaps there is something they like to do at home?

Writing lists is an important skill which will be useful to the children in several areas of their life in the future. We shall use the children's lists at school to talk about what the children like to do in their spare time.

_____and
child

_____
helper(s)

did this activity together

102 **Writing for a purpose**

Saturday mornings

What do you like to do on Saturday mornings?

● List three things you like to do sometimes.

impact WRITING HOMEWORK

Favourite books

Which are your favourite books?

- Write down five of your favourites – the title and the author. Draw a character from each of the books.

To the helper:

- Talk about the books your child enjoys the most. Is there a certain type of book that they prefer?
- Put the child's favourite book at 'Number One' in your list, and so on.

Writing lists is an important skill which will be useful to the children in several areas of their life in the future. We shall use the lists to talk about their favourite types of books.

_____and

child

_____

helper(s)

_____

did this activity together

impact WRITING HOMEWORK

Writing for a purpose 103

To the helper:

- Discuss the TV programmes your child enjoys the most. Is there a certain type of programme that they prefer?
- Write the list in order, with your child's favourite programme at 'Number One', and so on.

Writing lists is an important skill which will be useful to the children in several areas of their life in the future. We shall use the lists in school to talk about the favourite programmes.

_____ and
child

_____
helper(s)

_____
did this activity together

104   Writing for a purpose

Television favourites

Which are your favourite TV programmes?

- Write down five of your favourites, and draw a character from each one of them.

impact WRITING HOMEWORK

Review

Choose a film you have seen recently.

Would you recommend it?

- Write down three reasons why you think someone else should go and see it.

- Give the film a rating between one and five stars. Five stars for an excellent film, one for a terrible one!

impact WRITING HOMEWORK

To the helper:

- Talk about the most recent film your child has ever seen. Can they tell you the plot? Emphasise keeping the events in the correct order.
- Pick three good reasons that you could write down, and then award stars.

Recording a child's opinion of a film provides the children with a purpose for writing. In school we shall discuss the films that the children have seen, and the star ratings they gave them.

_____and
child

_____
helper(s)

_____
did this activity together

Writing for a purpose   105

To the helper:

- Talk about the meal that your child always asks for. Is it a meal that you eat at home, at someone else's house, or out at a cafe or restaurant?

Writing lists is an important skill which will be useful to the children in several areas of their life in the future. We shall use the lists in school to talk about the children's favourite types of food.

_____ and

child

_____

helper(s)

did this activity together

Meal ratings

What is your favourite meal? Give it five stars.

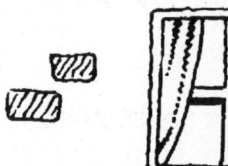

- Write down some other meals you enjoy and put them in order by the stars.

Can you think of a meal that you would only give one star to?

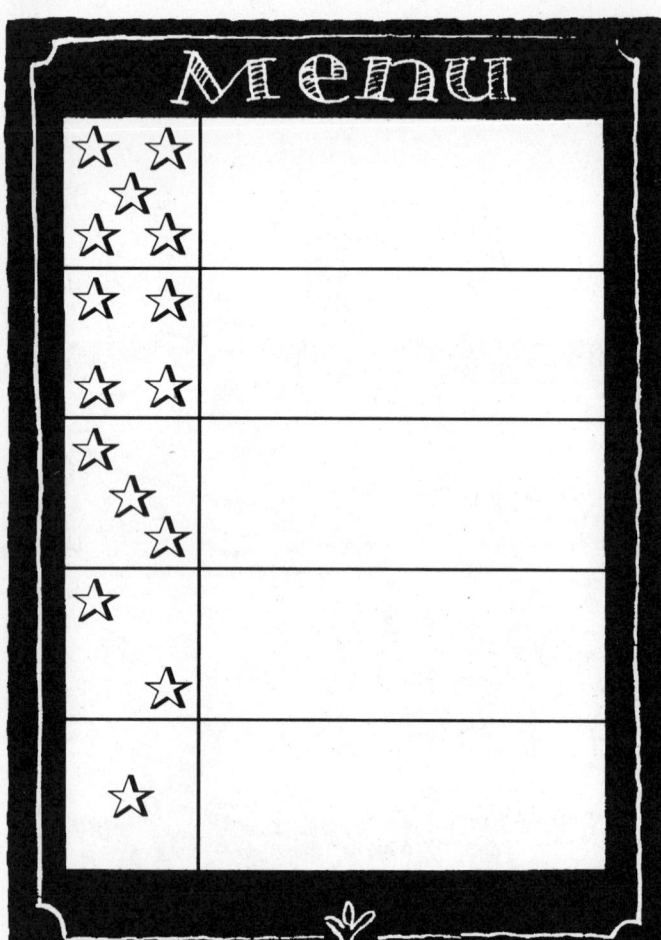

Menu

106 Writing for a purpose

impact WRITING HOMEWORK

Favourite games

- Write down a list of all your favourite games.

Think about all kinds of games: computer games, sports, card or board games.

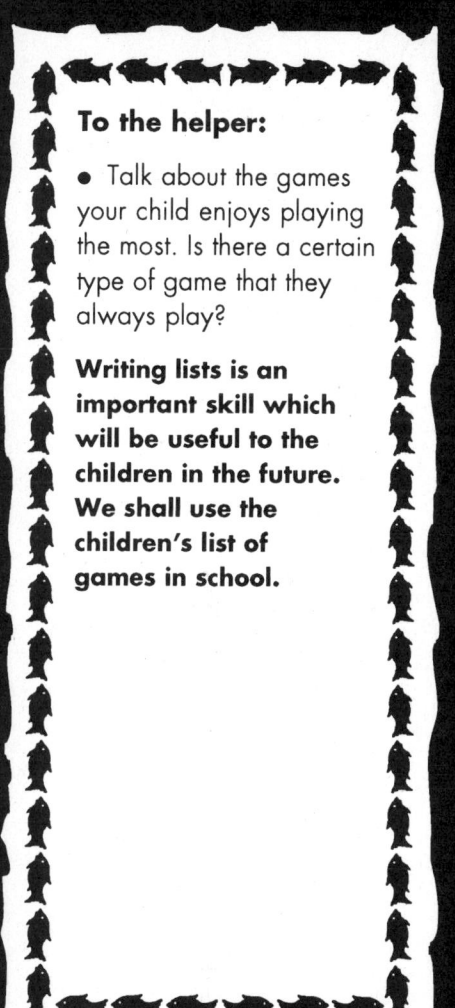

To the helper:

- Talk about the games your child enjoys playing the most. Is there a certain type of game that they always play?

Writing lists is an important skill which will be useful to the children in the future. We shall use the children's list of games in school.

_____and
child

_____
helper(s)

_____
did this activity together

impact WRITING HOMEWORK

Writing for a purpose 107

To the helper:

- Talk about your child's favourite toy. What is so special about it? Is it a recent acquisition, or has it been a favourite for years?
- It might help to look through a catalogue, or through some advertisements to get some ideas.

Writing adverts is one form of writing for a purpose. A certain message has to be communicated clearly, and attractively. We shall display the children's advertisements at school.

_____ and
child

_____
helper(s)

_____
did this activity together

108   **Writing for a purpose**

Top toy

Which is your favourite toy?

- Design an advertising poster for this toy.

What is its best feature?

- Draw a picture, and write some kind of slogan that will make other children want to buy it.

impact WRITING HOMEWORK

Be safe!

Do you walk to school or home from school when it is dark? What kind of clothes should you wear so that motorists can see you in the dark?

- Draw a picture of yourself wearing sensible clothes, with labels showing the important items of clothing.

To the helper:

- If you are a driver, talk to your child about how difficult it can be to see pedestrians in the dark. What colours show up well? How else can you make sure you can be seen in the dark?

Labelling a diagram provides the children with a purpose for their writing. We shall be talking about safety on the roads at school.

_____ and
child

_____
helper(s)

_____
did this activity together

impact WRITING HOMEWORK

Writing for a purpose

To the helper:

- Can you remember the Green Cross Code? Talk about the rules in the code, or sensible rules that you can think of.
- Number the rules in the order that you should do them.

Writing a set of rules will help the children really think carefully about an issue that is important to them and other children. They will have to set out their information clearly to communicate their ideas effectively.

_____and
child

_____
helper(s)

_____
did this activity together

110 **Writing for a purpose**

Crossing the road

When you are older you will be ready to cross roads by yourself.

Do you know how to cross the road safely?

- Write down five rules for crossing the road.

impact WRITING HOMEWORK

Ha ha ha!

Have you got any favourite jokes in your family?

- Write down one of the jokes.
- Illustrate the joke.

To the helper:

- Ask around the family for a joke that everyone laughed at once, but which still brings a smile to everyone's faces when it is referred to.
- Jokes can be quite long-winded, so do help with the writing if necessary.

Writing down a joke to share with the rest of the class provides the children with a purpose for their writing. We shall be sharing the jokes at school, and making a class 'Joke Book'.

_____and

child

_____

helper(s)

_____

did this activity together

impact WRITING HOMEWORK

Writing for a purpose 111

To the helper:

- Talk to your child about the different ways in which water can be wasted.
- Discuss how water gets to our homes – show them the pipes! What images might your child choose for a poster? Which words will be useful?

Posters and signs provide us with powerful reasons for linking words and pictures or images. We shall use these posters to stimulate a discussion and some more writing in class. We shall also make a lovely display!

_____and
child

_____
helper(s)

did this activity together

112 Writing for a purpose

Save water!

Water is very precious!

Leaving a tap on, or a hose running after it has been used is a waste of water. It might even mean that there is not enough water for everyone when we need it.

- Make a 'Don't waste water' poster. Draw a really good picture. Try to think of a snappy slogan!

More please!

- Write a short note explaining why you absolutely should have more pocket money!
- List all the reasons you can think of.

To the helper:

- Talk to your child about pocket money. Is it necessary? What sorts of thing would they spend it on? Help them to think of some reasons why they should get more pocket money!

Listing our reasons for doing or wanting something is an important way in which we can put our thoughts in order. This activity begins the process of using writing to help us 'think things through'.

_____and
child

_____
helper(s)

did this activity together

impact WRITING HOMEWORK

Writing for a purpose   113

To the helper:

- Talk to your child about what information someone finding the cat might need in order to return the cat to its home. Discuss whether the cat's name should be on the paper. What about a reward?

Writing information – especially about ourselves – is an important skill. This activity reinforces children's knowledge of their name, address and telephone number.

_____and
child

_____
helper(s)

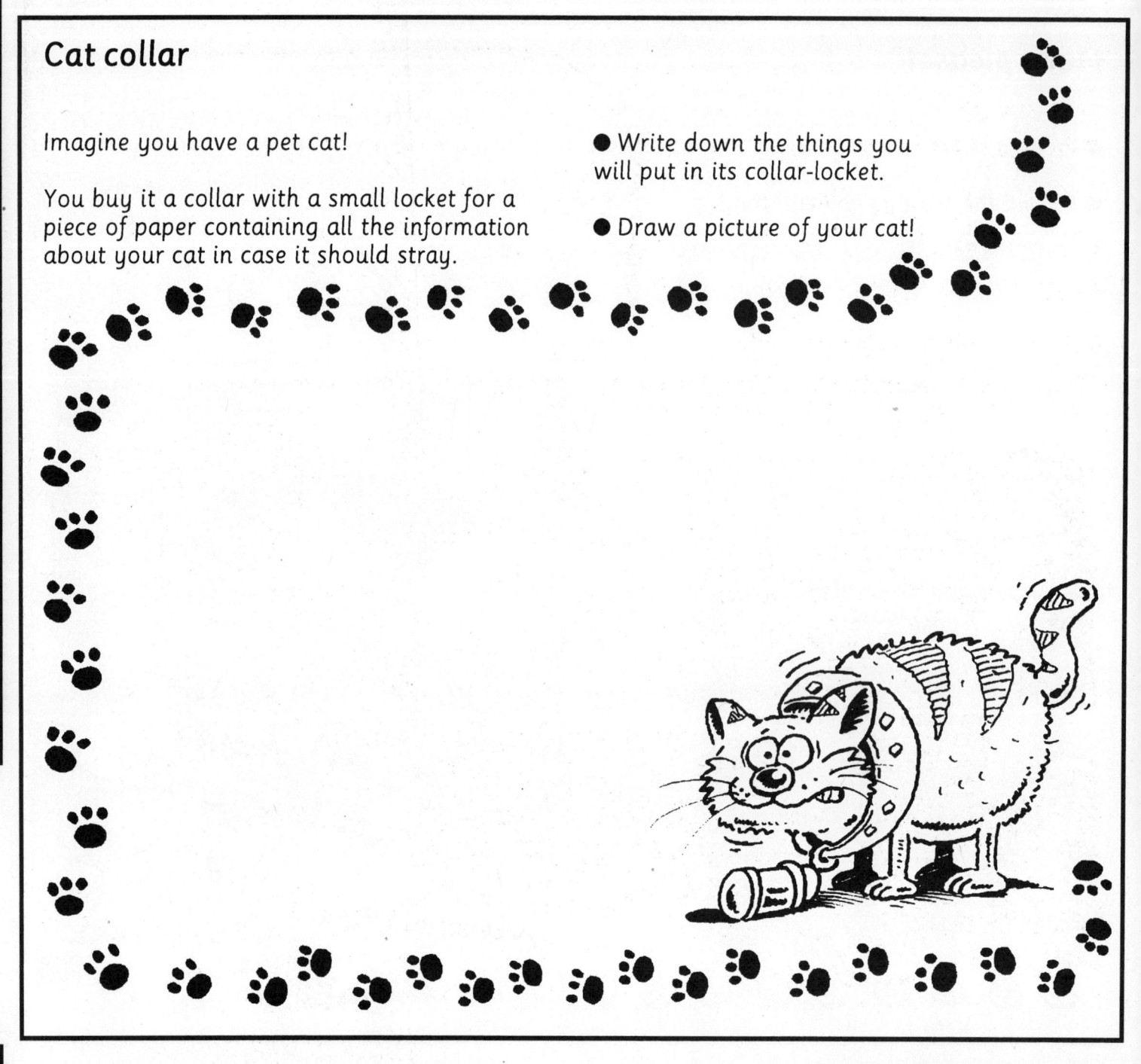

_____
did this activity together

Cat collar

Imagine you have a pet cat!

You buy it a collar with a small locket for a piece of paper containing all the information about your cat in case it should stray.

- Write down the things you will put in its collar-locket.

- Draw a picture of your cat!

Writing for a purpose

impact WRITING HOMEWORK

Luggage label

Imagine you are going on a journey.

- Write a label for your luggage. You must write your name and address.

Where will you go on your trip?

- Draw a picture of the place where you are going to.

To the helper:

- Talk about where your child might like to go! Discuss the sort of holiday they could imagine having – for example skiing, riding, sailing, to the beach or the mountains.
- Help them write their name and address correctly on the luggage label.

Writing our names and addresses is very important. We shall use the 'imaginary holiday places' to stimulate some further writing in the classroom around this topic.

_____and

child

_____

helper(s)

_____

did this activity together

impact WRITING HOMEWORK

Writing for a purpose 115

To the helper:

- Discuss outrageous excuses! Perhaps they are about to fly off into space, or a long lost uncle is coming to stay and he likes untidy rooms!

A note is a form of written communication which we use a great deal in modern life. Getting children into the habit of writing short clear notes is a way of extending their written skills.

_____and
child

_____
helper(s)

_____
did this activity together

116   **Writing for a purpose**

Excuses, excuses

Is your bedroom a mess?

● Write a note to someone at home explaining exactly why you cannot possibly tidy your room.

Make the excuse as outrageous as possible!

impact WRITING HOMEWORK

Can't go now!

- Write a note explaining why you cannot possibly go to bed when you are told to!

Make your excuse as outlandish as possible!

To the helper:

- Discuss outrageous excuses! Perhaps your child is about to go off to make a film! Or the Prime Minister is coming to see them about something very important.

A note is a form of written communication which we use a great deal in modern life. Getting children into the habit of writing short but clear notes is a way of extending their written skils.

_____ and
child

_____
helper(s)

_____

did this activity together

impact WRITING HOMEWORK

Writing for a purpose 117

To the helper:

- Discuss why they might not be able to eat something! Perhaps it has a frog in it! Or a long-lost starving cousin is about to arrive and this is absolutely all she will eat!

A note is a form of written communication which we often use in modern life. Getting children into the habit of writing short clear notes is a way of extending their written skills.

_____and
child

_____
helper(s)

did this activity together

118 **Writing for a purpose**

There's a frog in my porridge!

- Make up a really good excuse why you cannot possibly finish eating something you hate!

Make your excuse really persuasive – and as outlandish as possible!

impact WRITING HOMEWORK

Welcome here

- Design a poster welcoming children and adults to your school.

- Draw something on the poster which will make them feel welcome. Use some words which help express this message.

To the helper:

- Talk about the different ways in which we can say welcome.
- Discuss what your child can draw on the poster to make the school seem a welcoming place.

Posters and signs are a very useful way of combining the written word with a picture or image. We shall be looking at the children's posters and we will choose some of the best ones to go up in the entrance hall at school.

_____and
child

_____
helper(s)

_____
did this activity together

impact WRITING HOMEWORK

Writing for a purpose 119

To the helper:

- Talk about where you see 'Be quiet' or 'Silence' notices, for example, outside exam rooms, in hospitals or when babies are sleeping. Discuss the picture and the words which might go on their sign.

Signs and notices must be succinct and are clear ways of conveying information. This activity helps children to write in clear and concise ways.

_____ and
child

_____
helper(s)

_____
did this activity together

Silence

- Make a sign which says 'Be quiet'.

Think of a reason for being quiet! Where might you want to put up your sign?

120   **Writing for a purpose**

impact WRITING HOMEWORK

No free newspapers

● Make a sign to hang on a front door to tell people that you do not want any free newspapers delivered.

What should the sign say? Make it polite but clear. Can you make it funny as well?

To the helper:

● Discuss the advantages and the disadvantages of having free newspapers delivered. Think of a good idea for a sign – could it be funny? For example 'Our dog EATS free newspapers and gets sick... Please don't leave any here!'.

A notice or sign conveys its message in a quick and clear way. This activity helps children to focus on how to say something in as few words as possible.

_____and

child

_____

helper(s)

_____

did this activity together

Writing for a purpose

To the helper:

● Talk about how the sign might look. What picture should you draw? What words will the sign need to say?

A sign is a form of written communication which we use a great deal in modern life. Designing a sign helps children to think clearly about what they want to say.

_____ and
child

_____
helper(s)

did this activity together

122   Writing for a purpose

Shoes off!

Pretend it has been very muddy recently!

● Design a sign to tell everyone to take their shoes off as they come into your house. Make it clear – and funny if you can!

impact WRITING HOMEWORK

Ladies and gentlemen

- Design some new signs for the doors of the 'Ladies' and 'Gents' toilets.

Make sure it is clear which one is which!

To the helper:

- Talk about the signs that you see on toilet doors. For example 'Guys' and 'Gals' or 'Boys' and 'Girls'. Can your child think of ways of making the signs using pictures as well as words?

We shall make a display of all the children's signs. We shall also use this activity to start a discussion of synonyms (words which mean the same).

_____ and
child

_____
helper(s)

_____
did this activity together

impact WRITING HOMEWORK

Writing for a purpose 123

To the helper:

- Discuss what would be a good wish to have. Consider what makes you happy/sad. Remind your child that this is only one wish.

A note is a form of written communication which we use a great deal. Learning to write short clear notes is an important part of extending written skills.

_____ and
child
_____
helper(s)

did this activity together

124   **Writing for a purpose**

A wish, please!

Imagine that you have found a magic lamp!

But the genie can only understand written messages!

● Write a note to him telling him what your wish is.

impact WRITING HOMEWORK

Wake-up words

What words do you like someone to say to you to wake you up?

- Write down two or three of your favourite 'wake-up' calls'!

To the helper:

- Talk about how the child likes to be woken! Tell them how **you** would like to be woken! Help them to write down one or two suggestions.

Writing lists of ideas helps adults and children to think things through. This activity is part of developing these early list-making skills. We shall make a lovely display of 'wake-up calls'!

_____and
child

_____
helper(s)

_____
did this activity together

impact **WRITING HOMEWORK**

Writing for a purpose

To the helper:

- Talk about how the child likes to be settled to sleep. Discuss how you say good-night – perhaps in a language other than English?
- Help them to write down one or two suggestions.

Writing lists of ideas helps adults and children to think things through. This activity is part of developing these early list-making skills. We shall make a lovely display of 'going to bed words'!

_____and
child

_____
helper(s)

_____
did this activity together

Writing for a purpose

Good-night all

What words do you like someone to say to you last thing at night.

- Write down two or three of your favourite and comforting 'night-night sayings'.

impact WRITING HOMEWORK

Farewell my lovely

Pretend you have won a 'Round-the-world' trip!

- Make a list of all the different forms of transport you could use on your trip.

Be as imaginative as you like! How long can you make your list?

- Draw your favourite form of transport.

To the helper:

- Discuss all the different forms of transport. Remember to include the outlandish ones like camels and rockets, as well as mundane ones like trains and bicycles!

Writing lists of ideas helps adults and children to think things through. This activity helps develop early list-making skills. We shall make a lovely display of different forms of transport in school.

_____and
child

_____
helper(s)

did this activity together

impact WRITING HOMEWORK

Writing for a purpose   127

IMPACT schools

We are trying to compile a list of IMPACT schools so that we can:
- inform you as new materials are produced;
- offer help and support via our INSET office;
- find out the spread of this type of shared writing homework.

Also, because it is helpful if you have support and advice when starting up a shared homework scheme, we have a team of registered in-service trainers around Britain. Through the IMPACT office we can arrange for whole day, half day or 'twilight' sessions in schools.

I would like further information about IMPACT INSET sessions.

YES/NO

Please photocopy and cut off this strip and return it to:

The IMPACT Office,
Education Dept.,
University of North London,
Holloway Road,
London N7 8DB.
0171 753 7052

Teacher's name _____
School's name _____
_____
Address _____
_____
_____
LEA _____

Management

Most teachers send the shared writing task as a photocopied sheet included in the children's **Reading Folder** or in their IMPACT **Maths folder**. Remind the children that they may use the back of the IMPACT sheet to write on. Before the activity is sent home, it is crucial that the teacher prepares the children for the task. This may involve reading a story, going over some ideas or having a group or class discussion. Some ideas are provided here in the Teachers' Notes for each activity. The importance of this preparation cannot be overstressed.

Many of the tasks done at home lend themselves naturally to a display or enable the teacher to make a class-book. A shared writing display board in the entrance hall of the school gives parents an important sense that their work at home is appreciated and valued.

The shared writing activity sheets can be stuck into an exercise book kept specifically for this purpose. Any follow-up work that the children do in school can also be put into this book. As the books go back and forth with the activity sheets this enables parents to see how the work at home has linked to work in class.

Non-IMPACTers

We know that parental support is a key factor in children's education and children who cannot find anyone with whom to share the writing task may be losing out. Try these strategies:
- Encourage, cajole and reward the children who bring back their shared writing. If a child – and parent/carer – does the task haphazardly, praise the child whenever the task is completed, rather than criticise if it does not.
- If possible, invite a couple of parents in to share the activities with the children. This involves parents in the life of the school as well as making sure that some children don't lose out.
- Some schools set up 'writing partners' between children in two different classes pairing a child from Y6 with a child in Y1 for shared writing activities, perhaps weekly or fortnightly.

None of these strategies is perfect, but many parents will help when they can and with encouragement, will join in over the longer term.

Useful information and addresses

The IMPACT shared maths scheme is running successfully in thousands of schools in the UK and abroad. The shared writing works in the same way, and obviously complements the maths very well. Both fit in with the shared reading initiatives (PACT or CAPER) which many schools also run. The OFSTED Inspection Schedules require and take account of schools working with parents as well as the quality of teaching and learning. IMPACT receives positive mentions in inspectors' reports.

Further information about the IMPACT Project and IMPACT inservice training for schools or parents' groups can be obtained from: The IMPACT Project, School of Teaching Studies, University of North London, 166–220 Holloway Road, London N7 8DB.

The Shared Maths Homework books can be obtained from Scholastic Ltd, Westfield Road, Southam, Warwickshire CV33 0JH.

For IMPACT Diaries contact: IMPACT Supplies, PO Box 126, Witney, Oxfordshire OX8 5YL. Tel: 01993 774408.

Curricula links

The activities in this book support the following requirements for writing in the UK national curricula for English.

National Curriculum: English
1. Range – a,b,c
2. Key Skills – a,b
3. Standard English and Language Study – a,b

Scottish 5-14 Guidelines: English Language

Strand	Level
Functional writing	A/B
Personal writing	A/B

Northern Ireland Curriculum: English
Pupils should have opportunities to write in a variety of forms – including labels, letters, instructions, greeting cards and lists – and within meaningful contexts. Pupils should be taught:
- to structure sentences correctly;
- the names of forms of writing;
- to use connectives.